Please
shown.

Renew

Textph
spee

w

A Land Fit for Heroes

By the same author

THE BRIDGEWATER HERITAGE
MANCHESTER ALES AND PORTER

A LAND FIT FOR
HEROES

British Life after the Great War

CHRISTOPHER GRAYLING

BUCHAN & ENRIGHT, PUBLISHERS
LONDON

First published in 1987 by
Buchan & Enright, Publishers, Limited
53 Fleet Street, London EC4Y 1BE

British Library Cataloguing in Publication Data
Grayling, Christopher
    A land fit for heroes: British life
    after the Great War.
    1. World War, 1914-1918 — Social aspects
    — Great Britain   2. Great Britain —
    Social conditions — 20th century
    I. Title
    941.083   HN385

ISBN 0-907675-68-9

Picture research: Christopher Grayling
and Sophie Hartley

Set in Goudy Old Style
by Leaper & Gard Ltd, Bristol
Printed and bound in Great Britain by
Biddles Ltd, Guildford

CONTENTS

What is our task? To make Britain
a fit country for heroes to live in.

— David Lloyd George, 24 November 1918

ACKNOWLEDGEMENTS

Having received so much help from others in putting together this work, it is hard to know just where to start in acknowledging my debts to them. But I think my greatest debt is to what I consider to be the most fascinating book I have yet read, namely Robert Roberts's portrait of life in Salford in the first quarter of this century, *The Classic Slum*. It was my interest in his memories of life in the slums before the War, and his brief recollections of the impact of the conflict on the world in which he was brought up which led me to want to find out more. If I were to select a single source of inspiration for this book, then that would be it.

The bedrock of the material I have used to make up this book lies in the memories of people who lived through this period and who were kind enough to give over some of their time to recounting those memories for my benefit. They come from all parts of the country, and from all walks of life, and insofar as it is possible to be representative of a nation, then I believe them to be so. There are too many names to mention all, but in particular I would like to offer my thanks to Frank Mullineux, Phoebe Hesketh, Annie Turner, Elizabeth Mcleman and Thomas Barlow. I also am indebted to a few who did much to help me track down my sources, including Andrew Cross, the Salford City Archivist, The Venerable John Richards, Archdeacon of Exeter, and Celia Marshall.

I must confess, in one or two instances, to having drawn on already published material, where I felt that therein lay the best source material. In particular, I made extensive use of Frank Victor Dawe's excellent book, *Not in Front of the Servants*, and of Jonathan Gathorne Hardy's *The Public School Phenomenon*.

Nor could I have done without the assistance of the staff of the North West Sound Archive in Lancashire or the National Sound Archive in London. Alison Watson lent me a copy of her thesis on life in a Lincolnshire village which provided me with useful material.

I am also grateful to Jayne Moscrop and Nicky Dallen for helping produce the finished typescript.

Finally I must pass a word of thanks to my publishers, Toby Buchan and Dominique Enright for having sufficient faith in me to give this book their backing and to help me see it through.

PREFACE

The First World War was like nothing ever known before. Throughout history conflicts between nations had really been duels between small, professional armies, which had little direct effect upon the lives of ordinary people. This had begun to alter during the Napoleonic wars, but it was the outbreak of the 'Great War' in 1914 which really highlighted the change. When the Archduke Franz Ferdinand and his Duchess were shot at Sarajevo and a whole continent blundered into a war that no one really wanted, it was no longer a struggle between elites. Now it was entire nations which took up arms against each other. It was a change that was to have a profound effect upon the lives of ordinary people.

It is that change which underlies this book. The First World War involved every man, woman and child in this country, and tore many of their worlds apart, not just through the seemingly endless lists of casualties at the front, but also because of the way it changed people's perspectives on life. Those who went to the forces, and survived, together with the masses back home who helped on the land, in the factories or in the hospitals, came back having experienced an independence and a sense of participation that most had never known.

What this work hopes to portray is the world to which those people came back; its inadequacies, its changes and those things that remained the same. At the end of the War, the Prime Minister, David Lloyd George, promised that postwar England would be a land fit for heroes to live in. This is a picture of that land and of those who lived in it.

One is struck by how fondly those who lived through the years after the First World War remember an era that, in comparison to today, offered far less material comfort. Severe hardship was often common, and even the prosperous saw their lifestyle eroded by economic and social change. Nor were the aspirations of the ordinary people who fought in the First World War really fulfilled. Though the working classes saw a real improvement in their living standards during and after the War, it was just a little more of not very much in the first place.

And those who were prosperous not only saw their position decline in terms of money, but also saw the erosion of what they believed to be many of the best aspects of English life. Upstarts, who didn't know how one behaved, appeared more and more in Society circles, perhaps living off fortunes made from wartime industrial production.

But despite this, the 1920s was generally a happy era, mostly, I believe, because of the way the First World War destroyed the rigidity of the Victorian way of life. Those who could remember life before and after the conflict all seemed to detect a change in attitudes.

Indeed, Robert Roberts, in *The Classic Slum*, entitles the chapter on the First World War 'The Great Release'. The harsh reality of war had made everything else seem rather trivial: people stopped taking life quite so seriously.

Nonetheless, the twenties were a period of almost unprecedented industrial unrest. The General Strike was only one of a series of strikes that disrupted the country throughout the postwar years. Huge social gulfs remained. The well-off could be extraordinarily naive in their attitude to the rest of the population. One of the most telling comments I came across from this era was made by the hostess at an elegant dinner party attended by the Conservative leader Andrew Bonar Law during one of the many industrial outbreaks of the time. 'Tell me, Mr Bonar Law,' she asked, 'Just what do these people really want?' 'Perhaps, madam,' he replied, pointing to the servants and the magnificent dining room in which they were sitting, 'perhaps they want just a little of all this'.

Nor had the better off become less severe towards their servants. The Duke of Westminster's agent tried to pay a man returned from the trenches the apprentice's wage he had been earning when he had left for the War four years earlier. Middle-class women still expected their servants to be up at dawn, cleaning and scrubbing, and would berate them if the work wasn't absolutely perfect.

Yet I came across virtually no class resentment among people I spoke to. Whilst some found employers, landlords, and suchlike, distant figures, the bosses were always respected. Towards the end of the long and bitter coal strike of 1926 a few men at a mine near Wigan had given up the strike and gone back to work ahead of their colleagues, causing deep resentment. A large number of strikers gathered at the pit gate for a confrontation when the working men's shift ended. To make sure there was no trouble, the managing director and chairman of the colliery had to lead the working men home; even as adversaries in the dispute, they were still respected men, and there would be no trouble while they were around. The well-off and those in authority were still regarded with deference by those below them in the social scale.

It is also possible to exaggerate the degree to which Britain was divided by the years of industrial unrest that culminated in the General Strike. Certainly there was discontent and determination in these struggles, but there was little sign that the country was to be racked by revolution. When the great conflict did come in 1926, it was an abject failure, poorly led by trade union leaders who had little idea what they were trying to achieve, and beaten by a government which had prepared very effective contingency plans. There were plenty of serious outbreaks of industrial unrest, but these were no more than was to be expected at a time of economic uncertainty and rising unemployment.

And of course there is another, very different image of the years after the First World War. This was not only the era of the General Strike, it was also the time of the dance hall, and of the most famous dance of all, the Charleston. It was a time of youthful gay abandon, and of so-called sexual revolution — mild though it was by comparison with that of the last thirty years. It was the time when being young became fun, not just for the wealthy and privileged, but for everyone. Elders became more tolerant and young people more rebellious. For the first time, largely because of the advent of the cinema as a form of popular entertainment, the young became fashion-conscious, as they tried to emulate their heroes and heroines.

In the past, people have placed much signficance on the literature of the twenties, and particularly on the work, lives, and lifestyles of the so called Bloomsbury set, notorious for their rejection of many conventions, particularly through their practice of what was essentially free love. This in part accounts for what was perceived as the sexual revolution said to have taken place in these years. I have found absolutely no evidence to suggest that such attitudes were in any way reflected in the behaviour of the nation as a whole and were any more than the way of life of a tiny but conspicuous minority. There was a sexual awakening and a moral shift after the War, but it was comparatively innocent, and not like that of Bloomsbury group, which in any case I regard as irrelevant to a book such as this.

This is not meant to be an academic study, but simply a portrayal, as vivid and accurate as possible, of life in postwar England. Much of the work is based upon long conversations with people who lived through that era and who experienced both the difficulties and the happiness of those times. Their memories still hold the best images of life after the Great War — the best key to evoking and understanding an era now long gone.

But it should not be forgotten that there were some variations in the way of life in different parts of the country — though the similarities are much stronger — and the fact that this work is based upon the recollections of individuals means that the end product is perhaps more subjective than it might be in an ideal world where one could talk to endless people and devote a lifetime to what is a fascinating subject. But I do not apologise for this. There is no way that any one writer or volume could capture the entire life of a nation to a satisfactory degree. All any individual can ever hope to do is to open a closed door just a fraction so that the uninitiated can catch a glimpse of what happened beyond. I hope that this book can do just that. It is meant to provide, for those who do not remember, some idea of what England was like then. For those who knew these times, I hope it will bring back memories of their youth in an era which is fondly remembered by most of those I talked to. It is often said that the outbreak of war in 1914 marked the end of an era in British life. That is certainly true, though the changes brought about by the War didn't simply happen overnight. It is that which makes the twenties so worthy of attention, something which they have had little of, certainly by comparison with the vast amount that has been written about the years before the War, the so-called Indian Summer. Encapsulated in the life of England in the twenties are the roots of our modern, and far more liberal, way of life. But equally, there are still plenty of remnants of the nation of the nineteenth century and the Victorian mentality. The First World War didn't sweep the old world away. But when the boys finally came home, a new era had begun, and nothing would really ever be the same again.

INTRODUCTION: WHEN THE BOYS CAME HOME

If I should die, think only this of me:
That there's some corner of a foreign field
That is for ever England. There shall be
In that rich earth a richer dust concealed;
A dust whom England bore, shaped, made aware,
Gave, once, her flowers to love, her ways to roam,
A body of England's, breathing English air,
Washed by the rivers, blest by suns of home.
And think, this heart, all evil shed away,
A pulse in the eternal mind, no less,
Gives somewhere back the thoughts by England given;
Her sights and sounds; dreams happy as her day;
And laughter, learnt of friends; and gentleness
In hearts at peace, under an English heaven.

Rupert Brooke, 'The Soldier'

The First World War was the war that should never have happened. There was very little reason why a relatively minor dispute in the Balkans should have exploded into the greatest conflict of all time. And even when the blusterings and bumblings of politicians, diplomats and generals allowed Europe to fall into conflict, there was little reason to believe that this new war would be any worse than a thousand before it. A quick campaign followed by a diplomatic settlement, and the boys would be home by Christmas, was the general view.

But this was not to be. The Germans launched a fierce offensive, but were stopped on the plains of northern France too far from Paris to be in a position to force a diplomatic settlement as they had done in the last major European war, the Franco-Prussian War, a generation earlier. The two armies bogged down, and there they stayed. Casualty lists in the newspapers back home began to lengthen. People started to know someone who had died and gradually the realisation dawned that this just wasn't going to be another war like all the rest.

For four long and bloody years rival armies butchered each other in the trenches of the Somme, and on the plains of Poland until the Russians withdrew from the War at the end of 1917. The flower of English youth really did die on the French and Belgian battlefields. Young lieutenants, fresh from school, men who in other times would have been the bedrock of their country's future, could expect to live only a few minutes at the head of their men fighting in the trenches. Families, both rich and poor, lost not one but all their sons fighting for a cause that few really understood — and certainly not those who played football in no man's land at Christmas with their enemies, then returned to their trenches to resume a much deadlier game.

The tide of the War really turned with the arrival of American troops to join the Allied cause in 1917. By that time also the bitter immobility of trench warfare was beginning to be overcome by the increased use of the recently developed tank. The Allies slowly began to make headway and break out of the relatively small area of northern France and Belgium where the armies had been stranded for much of the past four years. In March 1918 the German High Command, knowing full well that the steady flow of American men and munitions across the Atlantic was tipping the balance against them, launched one final desperate offensive. For a few weeks they made steady progress, gradually pushing the Allies back towards Paris, though at a terrible cost to both sides. But then the Allied line held, and began to advance once more. The Germans were beaten, and they knew it, but the Allies had no will left to push the war on into Germany. Both sides had had enough, and on 11 November the commanders of both armies met in a railway carriage in the Ardennes and signed an Armistice. The four-year nightmare was over. But of the armies that went away to war more than eight million — 750,000 of them British — would never return. By comparison, the Franco-Prussian War in 1870, which saw the complete defeat of France, cost only 200,000 lives.

For a while the enormity of the nation's loss disappeared in the euphoria with which news of the Armistice was greeted. Scenes such as those described by an Exeter schoolboy were typical the nation over . . .

'I was at school when the Armistice came. The treaty was signed at eleven o'clock, and that was the end of school for that particular day because we were all let out to go into the City. It was an absolute riot in the centre, and they couldn't run the trams. They all had to come off because of the number of people who had come out. They held services in the Cathedral every hour, and it was absolutely packed. People were just standing there. This was the reaction, the relief that it was all over.'

Bells pealed in churches across the country, and people danced in the streets. Everywhere there was jubilation, and relief that it was all over after a four-year nightmare. There was joy too that the end had come with victory, but this was far exceeded by the fact that it was the end. The nation was tired of grief, and of the seemingly endless lists of sons, brothers, husbands and fathers who wouldn't be coming home. They were not forgotten — over the next two years just about every city, town and village in the country gathered the money to erect its own very personal war memorial — but for a time relief and celebration swamped all emotion of the more melancholy kind. Just about the whole nation began to party.

It helped too that everyone was feeling rather well-off, for a time at least. Families had seen their incomes double during the war years as mothers and sisters joined the munitions

When news of the Armistice came through there was dancing in the streets, such was the relief that it was all over.

The celebrations were, however, tinged with sadness. In towns and villages across the country public memorials were raised to those who would not be coming home.

lines, and fathers and brothers sent back their wages from the front. The wartime siege economy had meant boom conditions for industry at home, both because there was no foreign competition and because of the enormous demands of the war effort. As a result real wages rocketed, leaving even the poorest families with a much higher weekly income than ever before. Even before the soldiers began to come home, the pubs, clubs and dance halls were filled to overflowing with people trying to get the tragedies of the War out of their systems. Some were horrified by this apparent lack of respect for the dead, and wrote to *The Times* forcefully to say so.

But most people would have agreed with a member of the ambulance corps in France, demobilised soon after the Armistice. 'We all had', he said, 'an awful lot of catching up to do'. And they did a pretty good job of doing just that.

Whilst those back home were celebrating, much of the Army was kept intact for the best part of a year after the fighting stopped. Some remained in France, some in barracks in England. Others went on into Germany with the army of occupation, which took over parts of Western Germany under the postwar agreements. It was a time to reflect on the future. One veteran who went to Cologne with the occupying forces told of a loss of direction in his and his comrades' lives when the War ended. Particularly for those from humbler backgrounds, or who had no definite job to return to, there was a feeling of 'What now?' For many, the War had been a great escape from the drudgery of a working life in the slums, or from the hand-to-mouth existence of the farm labouring communities. At the front there might have been death and destruction, but there was also comradeship and a sense of purpose that many had never known before. The approaching end of that way of life left many very uncertain about their future.

There were, of course, those for whom the future held no mysteries. Durham miners, for example, were quickly weeded out of the army of occupation after the Armistice and returned home to ease the severe labour shortage there. And there were many others who had definite places to go back to, among them teachers. A schoolmaster from a small Lincolnshire town told how demobilisation had little effect on his life. His school was short of staff, and his return to fill one of the gaps was just like ending a long break away. Re-adjusting to school and civilian life, he said, was very easy for him.

For a government committed to providing a land fit for heroes to live in, Lloyd George's administration did a pretty poor job of winding up the war effort and maintaining morale as they did so. They took some steps which were inevitable and right, most notably making sure that all those who fought for their country would have a say in its future by extending the vote to all men over the age of twenty-one, and for the first time, to a limited number of women. Previously, only male householders had been able to vote. But their inept handling of demobilisation limited any popularity boost they might have won from the returning heroes. It took around a year to get all the conscripts home, which infuriated many of them. In parts of the army there was near mutiny — soon after the end of the War, for example, troops at Dover and Folkestone refused to embark for France. There was even some violence — Luton Town Hall was burned in protest at the way demobilis-ation was being handled.

This bitterness was wholly justified. Many of the war veterans literally did miss the party. For a few months after the end of the War the economy boomed. The continual cele-brations and the extra spending power of families and soldiers returning with gratuities of up to forty pounds in their pockets, gave commerce and industry a huge boost. For most of 1919 there were jobs for everyone, and the veterans who were allowed home were easily reabsorbed into jobs that were often far better paid than those they had left.

Those who came home last were less fortunate. The postwar boom lasted only until the end of 1919, by the autumn of which things had already begun to take a turn for the worse. There were fewer jobs around and it took longer to find them. As the 1920s began, the reality was clear: the past few months, when all seemed to be going so well and there was every reason to hope that the land fit for heroes had really come, had been little more than a mirage. The War had dramatically changed Britain's position in the world, leaving much of her industry with its back against the wall. It was not an auspicious start to a new decade. All the last few heroes had to come home to was a dole queue.

Amidst the
Dark Satanic Mills

A WORKING LIFE

Britain's wealth in the nineteenth century was based very much upon the fortunes of the textile industry. The ingenuity of inventors such as Hargreaves and Arkwright had launched the economy into the Industrial Revolution, years ahead of the other major world powers. Englishmen had made countless fortunes and their goods dominated markets worldwide. This became even more true as the exploits of adventurers and merchants gradually expanded the 'Empire', and opened up new markets for the manufacturers back home.

The zenith of Britain's industrial prowess was reached in the middle years of the century. From mid-century onwards foreign competitors improved their own industrial base, installing new, modern plants to compete with the British. The unrivalled dominance of Britain's industry was gradually eroded away. The textile industry in particular began, by the 1870s, to find cheaper foreign products challenging it in overseas markets, particularly in the valuable Far Eastern trading centres like Calcutta and Shanghai.

Throughout the last thirty or forty years before the outbreak of the First World War, British industry found it increasingly difficult to maintain its trading position. Many textile merchants were forced to diversify their trade into new products in order to sustain profitability, and there was considerable hardship in many of the textile areas of northern England. Even so, in 1914 Britain was still a prosperous nation, with a vast empire, and she enjoyed a very substantial share of world trade.

The First World War could scarcely have been more devastating for the economy and for the fortunes of British industry. The first, and most direct, effect of the conflict was felt within months of the outbreak of hostilities. The early exploits of the German cruiser *Emden* against British merchant shipping caused the imposition of new taxes on the merchant fleet to cover the cost to the Royal Navy of providing protection. Inevitably, this burden was passed on to the shippers using the merchant lines. Furthermore, the *Emden*'s success had a deeply depressing effect upon confidence in the export and import world as a whole.

The problem for traders was, however, to get much worse. As the War progressed the German U-Boats became increasingly effective against merchant shipping, seriously depleting the number of ships available to carry goods abroad and making those shipments which could take place both hazardous and often considerably longer than in peacetime.

Effectively, much of British industry was cut off from its markets. Not surprisingly, those foreign powers not so constrained by the War stepped in to fill the gap. This was particularly true in the lucrative Far Eastern markets, where Japan and America both took keen advantage of the problems facing British industry. Furthermore, in a country like India, which had always bought large amounts of British textiles, the wartime shortages did much to stimulate the growth of domestic industries.

The effect of all this was devastating for the mill towns of the north of England, and for other parts of the economy — such as the mining industry — which depended upon the steam-powered cotton mills to buy much of their output. When life gradually returned to normal after 1918 British traders found that overseas markets which had once provided most of their profits were now dominated by others, and that they faced a long struggle to re-establish themselves there.

But the effects of the War upon the domestic economy ensured that this would be a far from easy task. For four years Britain had been in a state of economic siege, with its industry booming as a result of the artificial period of high output providing goods for the war effort. During the War price levels rose very sharply, together with both profits and wage levels for workers in industry. As will be seen later, this caused a significant improvement in working-class living standards and in the wage expectations of workers. Not unnaturally, after 1918 soldiers returning from the front to their old jobs in mill and factory expected a reward substantially greater than they might have enjoyed before 1914.

For a few months after the end of the War economic activity was rather slow, but as the soldiers returned with their savings and a demobilisation bonus, and as the restrictions caused by the War disappeared, the postwar boom started. For a little over a year, domestic demand and the partial restoration of foreign trade, combined with the enormous wave of confidence and hope which swept the country after the Armistice and the Versailles settlement, ensured that industry worked overtime to keep up with orders.

But it couldn't last. By 1920, the economy had turned for the worse, and the postwar euphoria died away. And by now the real effects of the wartime changes were beginning to be felt. Increases in prices and wages had pushed the production costs of British industry up to a level out of all proportion with those of its rivals. In short, British business found it not only difficult to compete in and regain old markets, but also even to match the prices of foreign competitors. Not surprisingly, employers made determined efforts to bring down wage levels, provoking widespread unrest among the labour force.

The vast majority of men coming back from the War as the boom got under way were fairly easily absorbed back into industry, though often at the expense of women who had taken their place during the War. Indeed, in some places there were even temporary labour shortages. Many businesses worked round the clock, adding extra shifts through the night to keep up with the temporary scale of demand.

As the months passed, finding a job became less and less easy as economic reality began to return. By 1920 unemployment was increasing rapidly as recession set in. Even with an expanding system of social security benefits, it was a situation that was to disillusion many.

Even for those who remained in work, conditions in mill, mine and factory still left much to be desired despite a century's pressure from social reformers. Certainly there had been improvements. In the nineteenth century a twelve-hour working day had been commonplace. By the 1920s it was far from unknown, but most people worked much shorter hours. In 1918 the average working week was 54 hours — by the early 1920s it had been reduced to 48 hours. Some — like the coal miners — were working as little as a forty-hour week. Furthermore, fewer people now worked on Saturdays, which had once been a working day like any other.

Generally, men and women started work as early as six or seven o'clock (though some did start later) and would work through until late afternoon with a break for lunch. Often, though, the working day began long before the factory gates opened. Few could afford to do anything but walk to work, and this could mean a two-hour journey to get there. The daughter of a Yorkshire mill worker, then only a child, remembers how the tramp of the clogs in the street outside in the early morning acted like a clock to her as each group of workers passed — those who had the furthest to go first of all, through until the final group who only had to walk a few minutes to get to work. Naturally, this process was repeated at the end of the working day, with the result that many returned after what was effectively a twelve or thirteen-hour day, even though actual working hours were fewer.

Rewards for work varied enormously. In the East End of London, for example, men who began as young factory operatives remember earning as little as ten shillings per week, although rates were often higher than this for school leavers. A typical working man's wage would have been around thirty to forty shillings a week, from which would be deducted a few pence for union dues, if he was a trade union member, and for national insurance contributions. It was still quite rare for the ordinary working man in the interwar years actually to earn enough to make him liable to pay income tax, though more and more of the better off artisans were earning enough to do so.

At the top of the working-class wage league came the skilled artisans of industry, men like the cotton spinners of Lancashire, the shipwrights and engineers in the dockyards and the train drivers. It was not unknown for a cotton spinner, who controlled a spinning mule — the machine which spun the yarn — and oversaw the work of a number of operatives, to take home perhaps as much as twice or three times the average wage — perhaps as much as four pounds a week. But they were the real aristocrats of labour, known as that even to their fellow workers.

Such status was not obtained purely through skill and merit, but often through an element of 'Buggin's turn'. In the spinning mills particularly there was no clear ladder of promotion for the talented. Once in his job, a spinner might well hold it for the rest of his working life. Once he did surrender it, he would be replaced not by the most talented of the other operatives, but by the longest serving. That caused resentment among the best young men in the mill, who saw little prospect of rapid advancement. According to a Bolton man who began his working life in a spinning mill, it was enough to make him leave for a new job elsewhere in the industry. Many of his friends tried to do the same — though as unemployment increased, not all could find an alternative.

On the railways, too, there was a tendency for promotion to go to the longest serving workers, though there was much more opportunity for young men to fill in for missing colleagues, and gain valuable experience for the future. It was every young railway worker's dream to become a driver, working on the footplate of one of the huge, majestic loco-motives which pulled the main-line expresses. But to achieve that goal a boy usually had to start as a humble cleaner in the locomotive sheds. Here he might have to toil for years before the big break came, usually in the form of a short spell on the footplate as a relief fireman. Gradually, such opportunities would become more and more frequent until the job became a permanent one. Here he could come to terms with the footplate and perhaps eventually begin some occasional driving under the driver's supervision. Then would come official qualification, and perhaps finally the long sought after driving job. A lot of it was skill, but each still had to wait his turn. And that turn could take many years to come.

In the spinning mills, rather unusually, the mules were virtually independent entities. Although the spinner was directly responsible to management for the quality and quantity

The 1920s were a troubled time for the great mills of the north; even so, such massive factories formed part of the backbone of British industry.

of work produced, on his own machine he was very much the boss, even down to the setting and payment of wages. Operatives, instead of receiving their weekly pay packet from the mill office, were paid out of a sum of money given by the management to the spinners. Not surprisingly, this system had its drawbacks. Most spinners paid all their men's national insurance contributions out of the money received from the firm, but some were not as generous, and there was often acrimony over the amount of the total received by the spinner that was passed on to his employees. But no spinner could afford to be too mean to the operatives, since the weekly payment from which they all drew their wages, including the spinner who kept what was left after paying his subordinates, was based on the week's productivity levels.

Piece work was, in fact, relatively common in many industries, but most notably in the textile-producing mills. With money always short on a working man's wage, even with the relative increases of the War years, there was never any problem securing a high productivity rate from workers doing piece work. In textiles particularly this could lead to difficulties. In the weaving process for example, the loom operators wove on a frame which had been set up by somebody else. It was not unknown for an entire roll of material to be ruined because of poor workmanship in that setting up. Given that each roll could be a significant proportion of a week's work, an operative might have to depend upon the goodwill of a manager to avoid losing wages through somebody else's fault.

Generally, conditions of work were far better than those of the previous century, though by today's standards they remained poor. Safety precautions were not always good, and industrial accidents frequent, something which must have been dreaded by men working in more dangerous conditions; since state support for those in trouble was still limited, disablement through injury at work could be disastrous for a family. Coal mines still carried the highest risk in this respect, what with the hazards of rock falls, gas and the mine shafts. Accidents were common below ground, and one of the girls who worked at the pithead at Maypole Colliery near Wigan remembers regularly seeing injured men brought up from the coal faces on stretchers.

Often safety standards were poor not through any deliberate attempt or inefficiency, but simply through lack of knowledge. At one Manchester chemical works, described to me by a man who began work there in the mid-twenties, conditions were appalling by today's standards. 'There were various fumes around, like hydrochloric acid and sulphur dioxide, and the men worked in them without batting an eyelid,' he said. 'When the factory inspector came he just had a look round and nothing happened. There were no guards on the machinery to protect you from injury. And when men went home at the end of the day, it often took an hour or two for them to get their breath back because of all the chemicals they had breathed in. Nobody liked it, but they accepted it because there was nothing they could do about it.'

There was little overt concern, if any, about the adverse effects of workplace and work on the health of the employed. An elderly coal miner might fall ill with symptoms known to be common among men who had worked a lifetime in the pit, but this was merely remarked on. Nobody protested, not because of any particular subservience or reluctance to speak out, but rather because such things were accepted as part of the job: it was no good complaining or quitting, that was the way things were. Which is not to say there was a lack of interest in working conditions in the trade union movement. But that interest lacked the specialist medical knowledge of today, and there was too a tendency on the part of workers just to accept things as they were.

Facilities at the workplace were usually scant, and few factories had any form of canteen. Lunch was either brought from home by children or taken in each day as sandwiches. This in turn caused a problem, since there was not always anywhere to leave food while you were at work, and all too often lunch was abandoned in an unhygienic corner for the morning before being eaten. Many jobs were very dirty, particularly in the mining industry, yet virtually no workplaces had washing facilities for employees. At the pit head baths did not begin to become generally available until well into the 1930s, and many mines had to wait until after the Second World War for theirs. Children from mining communities at the time all remember vividly the havoc in the tiny cottages when father returned home and wanted to clean off the grime picked up during his day's work. In fact, some men didn't bother, preferring to wash only once a week, at the beginning of the weekend. In

Miners coming off shift at a Lancashire colliery in the 1920s. There were no pithead baths then — the men had to wash at home until the 1930s or later.

the meantime they only washed face and neck, so that the rest of the pit grime remained concealed underneath their clothes.

Not only was work both in the pits and in factories frequently dirty, but also, given the absence of any form of effective air conditioning, the temperature could be unbearably hot. Many worked stripped to the waist. Others discarded clogs and worked in bare feet, though often this could be difficult because the floors themselves got very hot, and in some factories there were slivers of sharp metal lying around.

Within the workplace discipline was often severe. In many places the gates were shut promptly at the beginning of the shift. Even when someone was only a couple of minutes late, they might well be shut out for the rest of the day, without pay. Hardly surprisingly, few were ever late. Workers had little or no protection against dismissal, even with the growth of trade unionism. This was particularly true where a business was still family owned, or dominated by a small number of men. Most of these businessmen belonged to the old school of employers who believed in absolute discipline and hard work. They ruled their businesses with rods of iron, brooking no nonsense from employees. A rule was a rule, and failure to keep it meant the sack. In reality, though, such stern steps were seldom necessary, since the boss was regarded with fear or awe. Few dared to step out of line and risk the loss of their livelihood.

At Maypole Colliery, in the area on the surface where most of the women worked there were two special tokens hanging on the wall. If anyone wanted to go to the lavatory, they had to take one of the tokens with them. However desperate you might be, if there was no token there at the time, you had to wait until somebody returned one of them. And if you didn't, the boss played merry hell with you.

But not all bosses were anything near to being tyrannical. Indeed, the attitude of many of them towards the workforce reflected the strong nonconformist heritage of this entrepreneurial class: while firmly believing in hard work and strong discipline, they were nonetheless benevolent. Workers at one Manchester brewery, for example, always received a couple of free pints of ale during the day to keep thirst at bay, and many smaller employers would often find an excuse to slip a little extra to the men, perhaps at Christmas or at holiday time.

Relations between workers and bosses often depended upon the size of the business concerned. Women who worked in the vast Bryant and May match factory in the East End of London, for instance, remember their employers as distant men with whom they had little contact. This was naturally truer in the cities than in the smaller industrial communities such as the mining villages. There, when the owners took an active role in the business, rather than delegating to managers (normally men risen from the ranks of the workers) then contact between owner and employees would be much stronger. Furthermore, there was a general respect for employers in the workforce. Although the twenties were a time of widespread industrial unrest, this did not affect the fact that, as a whole, men viewed the boss as just that. His position was seldom resented, unless he was excessively harsh. Today, retired workers look back, with a hint of affection, upon the old school of employer as a strict and strong man. He might have been hard to deal with, but he was a fair man to work for.

Of course they were not all like that. Some, as in any age, were ruthless and unscrupulous. Others were more dogmatic and ignorant. The managing director of one northern estate company used to take great delight in sacking people without any real reason. One cannot think of the troubles of the coal industry without remembering Lord Birkenhead's

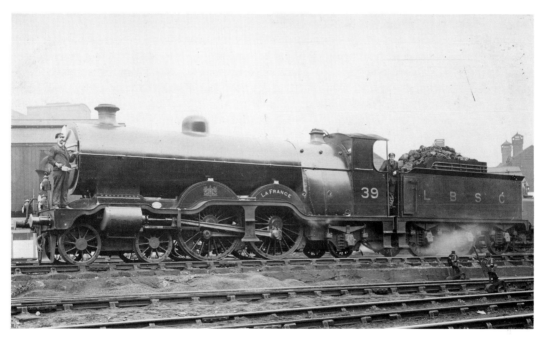

The railways inspired fierce loyalty and pride among their workforces. If a train stopped at a station, the driver would be out of his cab, making sure that his locomotive was brightly polished. Nothing else was good enough.

comment that he had thought the miners' leaders the stupidest men in England until he met the coal owners. But nonetheless it is fair to say that the average British worker, though often overworked and underpaid, still maintained a strong degree of respect for the man in charge, who paid the wages and whose word was law. And, as economic troubles led to increasing unemployment, you simply couldn't afford to cross him.

Furthermore, workers still maintained a great deal of pride in their work, even if they were on piece work. Most of all, though, this was true on the railways. Punctuality was vital: it was a matter of pride that a train should be exactly on time — not early, not late. Management demanded it, but the railwayman saw it not only as a duty but as a challenge. Equally, drivers and firemen regarded their locomotive as almost human. And indeed steam engines *were* remarkable machines. It was an art to know how to treat them, how to put the optimum amount of coal in the boiler for a steep ascent to be climbed successfully. If a locomotive lost steam, it took an immense amount of knowledge and skill to ease it into motion once more. Though a job on the railways was just a job in the material sense, for many it had something almost romantic about it. The smaller companies before 'grouping' (as it was known) merged the national network into four blocs in 1923, and the big four companies afterwards generally shared an enormous amount of corporate pride. There was a great concern for the appearance of the locomotive and rolling stock: brass was always highly polished, and if the train stopped at a station the driver or fireman would be out on the platform cleaning off any collected grime.

Such pride in work was far from being limited to the railways, though other jobs hardly fostered such sentiments. It would be understandably hard to work up enthusiasm for a coal face, but in such places as the fledgling car factories where there was a visible, tangible and attractive end product, morale and workmanship were usually good. Equally, where there was a corporate identity, as on the railways, workers took great pride in what they did. It was only with the onset of mass production that this began to slip away.

The gradual arrival of mass production in British factories from the early 1920s onwards was part of a general restructuring of British industry. Companies got bigger, and the smaller, more workshop style firms were slowly being superseded. This was mainly because of the nature of the new industries of the decade. Men like Henry Ford brought their large-scale industrial operations to this country, and set a trend which most moderate British motor manufacturers had to follow. Rolls-Royce and its like were able to continue building cars by hand, but in the medium-sized car range it was men, like Herbert Austin, who built their own mass-production lines who decided the future of British industry. The same was true of many of the other developments of the era. Both in Britain and elsewhere the chemical industry expanded into huge new factories run by new firms like I.C.I, which was formed towards the end of the decade. Another symptom of this move towards increased size and rationalisation was the grouping of the railways. Bigger, thought many, meant greater efficiency, and mergers and divergence into new fields within the same company became the norm. Though the trend towards rationalisation would be slowed by the onset of severe depression later in the decade, it was one which marked clearly the future of British industry and foreshadowed the great mergers of the 1950s and 60s.

Women at work lost out badly after the War as the soldiers returned. Many were given little option but to make way for the men and return to their traditional lives in the home. Sizeable numbers did nonetheless continue to work in the mills, in some factories, like the Bryant and May match factory, or even on the surface at the coal mines. Usually, girls worked for a few years prior to marriage. After that few remained employed, though in

Women never went down the mines in the 1920s, but many worked on the surface, mostly sorting good coal from bad.

some mill communities both husband and wife worked while grandparents cared for the children.

The pit brow lasses, as they were known, had long since ceased to work the mine itself; that had been eliminated by the efforts of nineteenth-century social reformers. Until 1926, many girls still worked with the banksmen, hauling coal out of the pit entrance and putting it onto conveyors. But it was hard work, and as the industry contracted and there were fewer jobs in the pits, this role was returned to men alone. This did not mean the end of women at the mines, though. Throughout the 1920s, and indeed up to the late 1940s, there were girls working on the screens, sorting out good coal from clinker and stone.

Generally, though not always, women were worse paid than men. It was rare for a man to begin his working life earning less than twelve or fifteen shillings per week, but both in the industrial heartlands and the East End of London, many girls started on only eight or nine shillings per week. It was unfair, but protests would have fallen on deaf and uncompromising ears. The days of equality were far off.

A further reason for the fall off in the employment of women in the years after the War was the appearance of a phenomenon totally unexpected and unknown for a generation, that of mass unemployment. It was to be a disillusioning experience for many ex-servicemen, though an improved dole system ensured that the utter poverty of the previous century would not be repeated.

In fact, if the Government had realised that high unemployment lay ahead, it probably wouldn't have been nearly as generous with its new provisions. During the boom it was decided to extend the scope of the 1911 National Insurance Act, which had set up a limited system of unemployment benefit for a few selected trades, to incorporate all industrial workers. Previously, everyone else had been forced to depend on the locally organised Poor Law system, which varied according to area and was generally less generous than the new national system. Now, at least, a worker made redundant could expect some money to keep him going, and only if the period of unemployment lasted a particularly long time would he be·forced back upon locally organised charity.

But the new scheme did not cover everyone. Many workers, particularly in deprived areas, still depended upon casual jobs for a living. Paying no insurance contributions, the onset of hard times for them meant the Poor Law and great hardship.

But above all, for a generation which had sacrificed so much in the sheer hell of the trenches, which had returned to a hero's welcome, unemployment was the destruction of dreams and the onset of bitter disillusion. An old soldier remembered meeting one of his former comrades in the docks in Bristol one morning as both hunted for any work that might be going. After all they had gone through, the other man said, the despair of redundancy and the lack of hope was just too much to bear. That same afternoon he hanged himself.

LIFE IN THE RED-BRICK STREETS

It has to be realised of course, that, despite all the hopes and plans, the quality and way of life could never have just magically changed, as people seemed to hope it would when peace finally came. The slums were still there, endless rows of terraces or back-to-backs, grey and dingy as they had always been, and often barely visible from above through the palls of wood and coal smoke from countless chimney pots. What Hitler's Luftwaffe would later do so successfully, the Zeppelins of the First World War could never have achieved. After the Second World War many of England's cities were ruined or damaged, letting the eager planners move in to devise a better future in their new towns and estates. But in 1918 there was no such likelihood. The slums stood and for those who lived in them there was little prospect of them ever falling.

The typical working-class home was invariably small and cramped, particularly if it had a large family to house. Two-up-two-down was a way of life. And modern comforts were almost non-existent, though it is fair to say that most of the luxuries we enjoy were yet to enter the inventor's mind. Very few working-class people had either hot water or electricity, and many did not even have gas to light their homes. And where there was gas, lighting often consisted of only a couple of gas mantles downstairs and tiny pilot lights upstairs, no more than a small flame coming out of a small pipe on the wall to pierce the gloom in the bedrooms. Those without gas had to reply on an oil lamp or two, or perhaps just candles.

Only the very upper echelons of the working class, the master builders and the highest paid artisans, who lived in newer, larger houses on the fringes of the slum areas where many of them had been born and bred, ever enjoyed the luxury of an inside lavatory. Most people were well used to the trek across the back yard to the outside closet. Although mains sewerage was becoming more common and many could enjoy the comparative luxury of being able to pull the chain, large numbers of homes still had the old earth closet with a cess-pool below. Once a week the local corporation would send round a cart to empty the sewage. Without the benefit of modern machinery and tankers, it must have been a singularly unpleasant task. There was, of course, progress in that by now the majority of homes actually had their own lavatory. But even this was far from universal, and in the worst and oldest areas it was not uncommon to find a block of closets serving a large number of surrounding homes.

Inside the home, conditions were primitive by today's standards. Often there was only

What the Luftwaffe would later do, the Zeppelins and Gotha bombers of 1914-18 never could have achieved. In 1918 the vast areas of back-to-back slum housing remained intact, and as drab as ever.

one cold tap to serve the whole house, usually either in the kitchen or in a small back addition. Hot water came sometimes from a large kettle on the grate, which was a permanent fixture in some homes. Or it could come from the big washing copper by the back door in which most clothes were cleaned. Underneath was a small grate used to warm water in the copper and to provide hot water for other household uses.

There is no doubt that for the woman of the slum home life was one of long struggle and toil, cooking and cleaning in cramped surroundings and striving to keep at bay squalor and what was ever-invading dirt. Cooking all had to be done over the fire or in the little brick oven at the side of the grate. It was a herculean task at times, and the older generation today express amazement at how their mothers managed. But manage they did, and by all accounts managed exceedingly well. Although the average family did eat better after the War than in Edwardian England, every woman still had to make a little go a long way. Feeding a hungry husband and a family at the end of a long day on relatively meagre resources was no simple task.

The food eaten by the average working-class family was still functional, though an enormous improvement on life fifty or a hundred years previously. Few went hungry, though the poorest families often had to make do with a diet of saveloys or bread and margarine, with a few extra 'luxuries' — perhaps a small joint of meat on a Sunday, and a bit of cheese or bacon. For the comfortably off, breakfast, an important meal because of the working day ahead, might consist of a bowl of porridge or a cereal, perhaps of 'Force', with the immortal Sunny Jim trade mark, and perhaps an egg with toast done on the fire. For many families there was only one main meal a day, perhaps at lunchtime if the husband worked nearby and could come home for a decent meal. That might consist of a stew cooked in a huge pot over the fire, with a bit of this and a bit of that — real hotchpotches

34

of ends of meat and miscellaneous bits of vegetables. Or else there might be the remains of the Sunday joint, which would often have to last well into the week. If the family had a good lunch, supper would only be bread and cheese or jam, washed down with tea. This was not a matter of choice. Working men had appetites just as great as today. Simply, the financial resources of many families did not allow for two good hot meals every day of the week.

Health in the slum areas was still a problem, but by comparison with the state in which many people had lived a century earlier, it was vastly improved. There were few serious outbreaks of illness, though from the last days of the War on into 1919 there was a severe nationwide outbreak of influenza which carried off many thousands of people. Even so, people were healthier than their ancestors, and most reached middle age.

Not that there was any lack of room for improvement, though. Proper health-care facilities were still relatively sparse, and those that there were had to be paid for. In fact it was not uncommon in the poor districts of towns and cities to find doctors who spent part of their time working for people who had no chance of paying for the treatment they received. Many employers organised sick clubs, to which a few pennies a week were contributed, which guaranteed the cost of treatment when necessary. There were also other collective ways of paying for health care, through local doctors' clubs, for example, and through health insurance schemes which were, theoretically at any rate, available to everyone. In practice though not everybody could or did join such schemes, and in any case many poor areas were deprived of proper local health care simply by the fact that there wasn't a doctor within reach. In an era in which the concept of free and universal National Health treatment lay twenty-five years in the future, many still did not receive the care they needed.

To make money go further many women did all their own baking in their little brick ovens, and many a family would never eat bread bought from a bakery. But there was little else that could be prepared in the home, and a sizeable part of every housewife's morning was spent shopping, eking out the few shillings she had to feed her family on for that week.

In most areas, shopping was a local affair, largely because most women had neither the time nor the money to go further afield. In many streets the little corner shop provided all, and a highly personal service to go with it, as a Birmingham housewife recalled. 'If you wanted cheese, the shopkeeper might break a little off for you to taste before you chose, or might let you smell the different types of tea on offer.' And for the weary or elderly there was usually a place to sit down while you were being served.

Personal recognition in the local shop could be a boon at the end of a pressing financial week before the wages arrived. Large numbers of families ran up credit during the week and paid it off at the weekend after payday. But there were some areas where the corner shop did less well, particularly where the Co-operative movement was strong. Where there was a good local Co-op supermarket the incentives offered and the range of items on the shelves made the extra walk well worth while. The key incentive was an interest scheme related to the amount of money a particular family had spent in the Co-op stores. When you bought your weekly groceries you were given a little paper check with the amount spent registered on it. Many families saved these up and at the end of each quarter received a dividend on the total amount spent. For many families the dividend was long-awaited; its arrival might allow the purchase of a new suit of clothes, or perhaps a much-needed item for the house.

But the corner shop always managed to survive, though perhaps less profitably than

Walkden Co-op, near Manchester. The Co-op stores were becoming more and more popular — they were cheaper than the corner shops, provided a greater choice, and offered a bonus dividend.

might have been the case without the supermarket and the attraction of the dividend. Indeed, within the working-class community it was far more than just a place to buy food: it was the focal point of life in the street, and an important centre of activity and the inevitable gossip that thrives on a very close-knit community. For that is precisely what those streets were. Each little area of an individual city or town tended to become a little village of its own, with its own social standards and hierarchy, often half cut off from the world beyond. Of course, the experiences of the War had broadened the horizons of many but, nonetheless, in the early 1920s these communities still remained largely as they had been before 1914. Some attitudes might have changed, but the soldier returning from the War would find the way of life little different to what it had always been.

Families dominated streets and local communities. It was not uncommon to find parents, children, cousins and brothers and sisters living in adjoining houses or in the same terrace. Most people had at least a few relatives in the vicinity. And of course in streets where people lived virtually on top of one another anyway, everyone knew their neighbours' business. And that of their neighbours' neighbours. Gossip travels fast.

But while these communities were close-knit, they could be less than harmonious and friendly. Even within groups whose living standards were essentially identical, there was a tremendous concern about respectability and social standing. Cleanliness was one important mark of status. Most housewives fought against tramping shoes and a dusty, polluted atmosphere to keep their homes spotless. One of the most scrubbed parts of the house was the front doorstep. It was, after all, the most visible part of the family home, and in a world where cleanliness was given such importance, apparent dirt might mean a step down on the social ladder.

Equally, possessions were a mark of standing. Every trinket that could be put on the mantlepiece, or picture that could be hung on the wall, conveyed respectability to the visitor. One particular social plus was the ownership of a piano. So much so that at the end of the War, when soldiers were returning with end-of-service bonuses, and people generally were more prosperous than ever, with their wallets fattened by the rich rewards of hard work in wartime industry, the Government had to put an *ad valorem* duty on pianos to prevent people wasting money on them purely to enhance their social status.

Often snobbery existed not so much within one individual community, but between different areas. This was particularly true in East London where, for example, people from Stratford remember looking upon those from Bethnal Green as being rather low and inferior. In most industrial cities, though, this attitude was to be found. There were the poorer streets, perhaps with older housing, in which the lower end of the working class lived. To the slightly more prosperous these streets might well be as remote as the large houses where the well-to-do lived. This pattern of social life was reflected in public houses. There were up-market inns where the artisans and the small employers might go, and small pubs in rougher areas where the labourers went, with a wide social range of locals in between the two extremes. And never the twain did meet.

And of course these distinctions were often based on some degree of reality. There were areas of partial destitution, of miserable, out-of-date housing, where people were semi-dependent upon casual labour and the poor relief still offered by the local Boards of Guardians, since not all the population by any means were covered by the expanded system of national insurance. In the last resort there was still the workhouse, a surviving relic of the Victorian era. The 'bastilles', as the horrified poor had nicknamed them a hundred years earlier, were on the decline, and after 1929 they disappeared, mostly converted into hospitals and other institutions. They were more common in the country-side than in the towns, and by now the more progressive and publicity-minded Boards of Guardians, the committees of local worthies who administered local relief to the needy, had renamed the old workhouses. But although conditions within were now far from Dickensian, they still remained a major deterrent to poverty and a nightmare, albeit distant, to those slipping down the social ladder.

Within these institutions there were no longer the barriers and conditions of the previous century. Husband and wife were now theoretically allowed to live together there, though in reality few couples ever had to resort to the workhouse. The inhabitants in the 1920s were made up of the disabled who could not get work, the unemployable and the wholly destitute, all outcasts from the slum world for whom nobody had any use, and for whom there was nowhere else to go.

But generally, even in the poorest of communities, people managed to muddle through, often with the charitable help of the more enlightened middle classes who came into the worst slums to help the inhabitants, and of the Poor Law administrators. And within these small areas, remnants of the more general social malaise of the previous century there was still warmth and friendship. At a specially established tea kitchen selling tea for a halfpenny a cup to the destitute of a district it was not unheard of for one man with only a penny in the world to share it with a comrade who had none so that both could have a cup of tea. Even ordinary working-class folk struggling to make ends meet in their two-up-two-downs could be shocked by conditions of life on their doorsteps if ever the twain did meet. But that was seldom, and in reality the destitute and the impoverished, and the families in their spotless homes in the little slum streets were in different worlds.

Street life in the slum areas was dominated by matriarchs, the older women who congregated daily to discuss local comings and goings, and to mull over social standings.

Street life in the slum areas was dominated by matriarchs, the older women who congregated daily to discuss local comings and goings, and to mull over social standings. Signs of hardship or behaviour unconducive with respectability were quickly noted and such news spread like wildfire.

Yet the closeness of life did not by any means simply breed malice and hostility. The fact that everyone knew everyone else's business did not necessarily have a negative effect, or serve only the whims of the gossips. If people got into trouble, whether financial or otherwise, then there would always be neighbours ready and willing to help out. Usually the close proximity of much of one's family was sufficient, but surrogate family was always close to hand. One Manchester woman remembers being fed each lunchtime by neighbours because her mother had to work full-time in the mill.

But it was the real family which filled most gaps. Often a woman would work in the mill for the whole of her young life, barely taking time off around the birth of her children. During the daytime children not at school would be looked after by grandparents. Equally, although there had been some degree of pension provision for the elderly since 1908, in the main the old were able to keep going because of the close-knit family structure and the strong loyalties within it. Where the old had no family, they were often to be found living in abject squalor. A priest from Shrewsbury who began work in the Potteries remembers finding an old lady living in a tiny room upstairs with half the stairs broken or missing, with virtually nothing to eat.

Nonetheless, the concept of respectability did permeate even the family structure; many families had 'bad eggs' with whom they had little to do, for whatever reason. But it was a concept that was beginning to break down. The catalyst was the War. Wartime England had been an era of prosperity for most. As we have already seen, because the economy was on a siege footing, industry was working as hard as possible. There was employment, and with it higher wages than ever before.

The result was that many of the residual poor of Edwardian England, people who had drifted from casual job to casual job, who had been in prison or the workhouse, and who had been amongst the most reviled targets of the matriarchs in the corner shop, suddenly gained an unprecedented degree of respectability and financial prosperity. Once gained, they were slow to let it drop. And by the time, in the early 1920s, economic conditions reached a point of such severity that one might have expected a new class of residual poor to emerge through destitution, unemployment pay had become sufficiently widespread to cushion the blow.

Equally, the younger generation simply didn't care for the standards of their parents and grandparents. The more rebellious and less conformist youth of the twenties, discussed in greater detail in a later chapter, were far less inclined to follow the conventions of the communities in which they lived. The War also served to broaden the minds of some of the older generation, though not all. Many men who had gone away to the War as tyrants, dominant in their own home and feared by wife and family, came back from the trenches much more relaxed and tolerant in their attitudes. Robert Roberts recalled one-time Lords-of-the-home who were now much more inclined to be comrades than rulers. Their horizons broadened, they were far less inclined to be petty and patriarchial. Husbands who had driven their wives to despair over what they would or would not eat, would now try anything at dinner time. Children who, without a father's belt to restrain them, had run amok in wartime, and had dreaded the return of their soldier parent and the strong discipline that might arrive with him, found instead that he was more inclined to laugh and tolerate, to say 'boys will be boys'.

Women were becoming more liberated. After years working with munitions, earning money and running their own homes, they were less inclined to conform to what had always been done. The War had broken down barriers which once seemed insuperable, yet now were half-forgotten.

But, despite all this, one cannot emphasise too much that life in the slums was still much the same. You could change attitudes, but the bricks and mortar and the living conditions did not change that much. In 1918, despite the improving wage levels from the wartime industry, the outbreak of influenza could still carry off thousands of people of all ages right across the country. Without doubt this toll was at least in part caused by malnutrition resulting from the shortage of many basic foodstuffs in the latter days of the conflict. But it was still a pointer towards the poor state in which a fair part of working-class Britain still lived.

Women who had found an unprecedented degree of liberation during the War found the work which had provided those new freedoms disappear as the boys came home and economic reality brought some sense back to the job market. It was the men who worked, and although in some of the northern communities women continued to work on the looms while grandparents or neighbours cared for their children, the vast majority ended up once more as housewives, working a seemingly endless day to keep their little homes spick and span and trying to keep families nourished.

Not that the lives of most men were much more rewarding. The only real retreat for most was the pub; still, at least they had that, which was more than the women and children had. National statistics for drunkenness showed a general decline across the country, but it was still rife. Often it was tragic. On a Saturday night, after closing time, many wives and families faced the wrath of a drunk and disillusioned individual. Many more bore the scars of that fate. Sometimes the drunken scenes were more comical. One girl brought up in a two-up-two-down in Salford remembers a regular ritual in her street each Saturday night when a neighbour came home from the local pub. Within minutes of his return, invariably, and for no particular reason, the kitchen table would be thrown out into the street. Neighbours would rise from their beds and with noses pressed to the glass would watch with amusement to see how much more difficult it was to get the table back into the little house than it had been to get it out in the first place. Saturday-night scenes, whether amusing or tragic, were commonplace in the working-class areas.

Yet, though the matriarchs might tut-tut, such things seem to have been tolerated. The next day, dressed in Sunday best, the drunkard of the night before was apparently accepted as normal again. Unless one stepped greatly out of line, social stigma was not that easily conferred. Everybody does seem to have been very friendly, certainly by the standards of today's impersonal world. Doors were never closed and a welcome was seldom lacking. Neighbours often treated each other's homes as their own living rooms.

This mentality was helped by a comparative lack of crime in the slum streets. Certainly there were offenders, and theft and crimes against the person not uncommon, but it was the better off who feared the burglar, not the slum dweller. In the terraced row you would have had difficulty in finding a locked door at any time.

The drive for some degree of respectability in the slums manifested itself most clearly on a Sunday. On the Lord's day everyone dressed up to the nines. The best linen would be brought out in the home — there might even be a lace tablecloth as father carved the Sunday joint. It was all very escapist — an apparent attempt to dissipate the mucky reality of a working man's life and to forget the gruelling task of keeping home clean and family fed. You put on a mantle of respectability and pretended just for the day that you were really quite affluent and enjoyed a decent place on the all-important social ladder.

Yet it was often all just an illusion. For many of the poorest people grim reality returned on a Monday morning when all the Sunday best was packed up and taken back to the pawn shop where it would spend the week, only to be recovered in time for next Sunday's daydream.

Church on a Sunday was still common, although censuses had shown that for a century congregations had been slowly declining, and many who did attend a service did so not out of sincere conviction but because it was both a socially acceptable thing to do and because there was actually little else to do on a Sunday morning. In fact, people often went to church more than once during the day to pass time, to be actually doing something.

Throughout the nineteenth century there had been a fierce divide between Church and Chapel, between the established Anglican church and the nonconformist movement. And though this had largely disappeared with the general decline in church attendance, it did still manifest itself on occasions. Within the community there was no longer a social divide between chapel-goers and churchgoers, except on very rare occasions. But the two institutions often took delight in scoring points off each other on a local basis, even in trivial matters. On one occasion two religious parades, one from church, one from chapel, met in the streets of Salford and, by closing ranks, did their utmost to block each other — while, of course, maintaining the solemn dignity of such an occasion.

If much of the zeal had vanished from religion and church life, one aspect of that life still played a very important part in the lives of many of the working classes: since their

Though the religious fervour of a century earlier had waned, the church or chapel remained an important focal point in the community, and religious parades were treated very seriously. Here, a 1920s vicar of Walkden leads his flock in a procession.

inception in the late 1700s, Sunday schools had been far more than just a means of bringing up children within the churches. They had become as much a working class as a religious institution. There was plenty of middle-class participation in Sunday schools, but it was as a way of becoming involved in the community. The middle classes did not need the Sunday schools, but their involvement was crucial to the schools' success. The schools were a quasi-community centre in which both parents and children could become involved, providing leisure for a class which generally lacked it. Certainly after 1918 this continued to be true. Apart from the educational aspects of the schooling they provided, of which more later, the Sunday school was a place for the whole family, where adults and children alike could find something to keep them busy. On Sundays they were schools, but during the week they became a leisure and self-improvement centre for all.

Where a working-class family did have leisure interests outside the home, the chances were that the organisation behind them would be the Sunday school. The school might well have its own sporting facilities, or at least have teams which played elsewhere. Non-sporting activities such as amateur dramatics and music were organised throughout the schools. It was not that they were, in themselves, miniature leisu
acted as working-class clubs giving people of all ages the opportunity to get together, to participate and to organise.

Of course, many ignored the presence of the schools altogether, either making their own amusement or simply drinking or sitting aimlessly through leisure hours. Membership of the Sunday schools was far from universal, and only a minority of adults were active in them. But for those who wanted to use the opportunity to make more of their leisure, they were invaluable.

There was also a rather different reason for the high popularity of the school's Sunday

41

classes amongst children, or rather amongst parents. Hardly surprisingly, in the cramped living conditions of the two-up-two-downs, those with families had little opportunity to be alone, and even less to have a satisfactory sex life. But on Sundays all was different. Sending the children off for part of the day provided that opportunity to be alone, and vast numbers of parents took eager advantage of it.

But many adults made little attempt to occupy their leisure hours. One favourite Sunday afternoon pastime was just sitting, watching the world go by, on a chair outside the front door of the home. And many a working man, perhaps when times weren't so good and pub visits had to be limited, would pass a summer evening in the same way.

Some families did make their own evening entertainment. One enterprising working-class father turned the kitchen table into a table tennis table, though the size of the room left little room to play. Families would play all sorts of indoor games: ludo, quoits, darts, anything either cheap or which could be improvised.

But for the older generation leisure was at a premium. Lighting was short and the working day began early, so evenings were not long. Father was often exhausted after the day's work, and mother had far too much to do to think of stopping to play. The more apathetic, those who didn't want to involve themselves in Sunday school activities or in the clubs and societies which did exist in working class England, really did do nothing but eat, work, drink and sleep. And on a Sunday they'd sit and watch the world go by, or spend all day in church.

Before the War only a very small number of the working classes were ever able to go away on holiday, not just because of financial shortages, but also because they simply did not have time off from work. But by the early 1920s it was becoming more common for the slightly better off families to be able to get away every now and then. They went to resorts like Blackpool and Skegness, or to places like New Brighton on Merseyside which expanded specifically to cater for relatively local holidaymakers. They could also sun themselves on the beach, watch Punch and Judy shows on the promenade or on the sands, and after a meal in the boarding houses where most stayed, perhaps go to a show or a concert.

But the holidaymakers remained the minority, even though their numbers were steadily increasing. Most people still had neither time nor money to take trips away — a Sunday in the countryside was a major trip for many.

There was a new world of leisure in the twenties. More was happening than ever before. But it was a world which belonged to the new generation, to the boys that came home and those too young to fight. The older generation, often even those who had fought in the War, belonged to the old era, to the Victorian and Edwardian England. Ultimately, life in the vast industrial conurbations of the country would be changed. But the experiences of the War could alone not do so, since whilst the younger went to fight and to make munitions, the old street hierarchies and way of life remained. The men worked and drank, and the women worked and gossiped. But it was not a life which the next generation could have adapted to. Contrary to some popular belief, the 'roaring twenties' were not just the property of the affluent: they were the property of the young.

SCHOOLDAYS

Most slum children were blissfully unaware of the world outside and of any concept of social differentials. Their world was a simple one, made up of school and games. Life generally was uncomplicated. In the playground richer and poorer mixed freely and unconsciously. With the prospect for most of a future in pit or mill, or scrubbing and cooking, of long hours and little rest, it really was true to say that for most these really were the best days of their lives, perhaps the only good ones.

In those days school began at five at the local elementary school and continued through to the official school leaving age of fourteen, except for those few who went on to a grammar school. Here the working class mixed uniformly, since unless you could afford private education, at primary level everyone went to the local school. The richer kids from the lower middle-class families who lived by the park in the bigger houses were taught alongside the poor relations from the worst slums. But there were no school uniforms, so you could always tell who was who.

Children still went to church schools, but the fierce divide between different religions in terms of schooling had long gone. A hundred years earlier the protests of Non-conformists or Anglicans about educational reform that might alter the religious teaching their children received had ruined the efforts of many educational reformers. By the 1920s, though there were denominational schools still, and children from, say, a Roman Catholic background might well still go to the local Catholic school, childrens' education was no longer as concerned with religion as with other subjects. Church school or no, the young were taught much the same everywhere.

The chief emphasis in elementary schools was on the three Rs — reading, writing and arithmetic — with a little basic history and geography, and perhaps some basic science if the teacher knew any. For one teacher taught all subjects — which may not seem particularly unusual until you consider that the elementary school was the one at which perhaps eighty or ninety per cent of children received their entire education. Today everyone gets the benefit of some specialist teaching as they grow older. For most pupils in those days there was none whatever.

Many schools also retained the rather antiquated system of teaching three or four classes in one enormous room. One class might be at one end, another in the middle, and a third at the far end, each receiving its own individual lesson simultaneously with the others, and each from an individual teacher. It was a far from satisfactory system, dating back into the previous century, and made life very difficult for teacher and pupil alike. Concentration, with the noise of other classes right alongside, was far from easy. In one classroom there

In the playgrounds of non-private schools, children mixed freely and without social restraint, whether their parents were artisans or unemployed.

In some schools, two or three forms might be taught in one room. Under those circumstances discipline had to be rigid. Granton Road School in Wandsworth, 1929.

might be up to 150 children. Such conditions needed strict discipline and regimentation where there were so many being taught at once; pupils had to learn to leave silently so as not to disturb the rest. Most classes knew the drill to perfection, and never made a sound.

One other relic of nineteenth-century schooling was also on the way out: by the 1920s very few children still worked on a slate in the classroom. Instead, the vast majority now had access to exercise books. Slates were in use only in places, mostly in small country schools and seldom in the towns.

The school day was much as it is today, although many children went to school on Saturday mornings also. One key difference, though, was the lack of any provision for lunches at schools. Most children went home for their midday meal, often walking more than a mile and back in the space of an hour's lunchbreak to get some food. Others were less fortunate still. In many places where fathers did piece work, and so couldn't afford a lunch break, children might be called upon to take a hot meal over to the works as well as to find time to eat their own.

Discipline in the elementary schools was harsh, as indeed it was in virtually every school at the time. Children were expected to obey rules and orders, and if they didn't punishment could be swift and severe. Corporal punishment was very much the norm, and could be brutal. At one primary school, on the edge of Manchester, the headmistress kept a huge and agonising knotty cane in her room to deal with miscreants. According to a woman who was at the school, but never actually suffered a beating from the headmistress's cane, it was a very effective deterrent. Those who suffered it once never came back for more.

But whilst virtually every school thought nothing of using brute force to instil discipline into its pupils, those children were in the first place much more obedient than they are today. In the words of one schoolgirl of the time, 'We'd never have dared do half the things the kids get away with today'. Even though father mightn't be the tyrant he'd been before the War, he was still strict at home. Children might be tolerated more, but they still risked a beating if they stepped out of line. And that in turn made the schoolteacher's job a whole lot easier.

Of course there were also practical difficulties which made firm discipline essential. In those classrooms, for example, where three different groups of pupils were taught simultaneously by different teachers, it was vital for the children to be well behaved, and if they weren't, for them to be brought quickly back into line. Otherwise the whole system would have been intolerable.

Elementary education was principally aimed at an exam taken by most children at the age of twelve to see if they could gain entry to the local grammar school, and, more importantly, to win a scholarship that would pay the tuition fees such schools still charged. Few were expected to pass, though, and even fewer actually did. Secondary education was still very much a preserve of the middle classes, with exceptions only being made for the brightest of the poorer children, who won scholarships, and those whose parents somehow managed to pay the fees.

The majority who didn't make it to grammar school stayed on at elementary school until they were fourteen. Some more progressive schools introduced one or two new subjects, such as basic algebra, into the curriculum for older children, and there were also more practical classes. But essentially it was just two more years of the same, finishing off an elementary education that by the 1920s was a right for all, but which proved of little direct help to most of those who left aged fourteen. For them a hard, manual working life lay ahead. The best days of their lives were drawing to a close.

Outside school, the streets were the poorer children's playgrounds: a street scene in Millwall in the 1930s.

Away from the classroom, the life of the young child was infinitely more varied and interesting than that of drudgery and toil suffered by his parents. At the end of the school day there was no homework, and few chores to be done, as often mother was only too glad to have her family out of the way while she cooked or washed.

Outside, the street became the children's playground. Most slum streets saw little or no horse traffic, and a car was unheard of. So there was no question of a safety problem. Groups of boys used the narrow streets as football fields, acting out the skills of their heroes on the real pitches. Many of the later great professionals learned their skills in the narrow, cobbled streets in the slums. Of course they had to be careful, they couldn't afford to antagonise parents with their games — father was still to be feared if he became angry, and his belt could be fearsome. And, strictly speaking, football in the streets was illegal. Although many policemen turned a blind eye, you couldn't afford to take chances when there was a possible fine of five shillings — a fortune for every small boy. Imagine how many bullseyes and gobstoppers you could buy for that kind of money. So there was always a lookout, and at the first sign of a uniform the cry went up, and little boys and footballs scattered in all directions. For many, playing lookout became quite a useful way of earning a few coppers to supplement the weekly sweet-buying budget. If children were given any pocket money by their parents — and not all parents could afford to — they only got a few pennies a week at most. Sixpence was a fortune to a child. On many street corners groups of men still gambled illegally, and they had more to fear from the police than the young footballers. Normally they were only too keen to pay some lad to keep an eye out for the law while they played.

In the working-class areas boys were always out to earn more money and sweets. Children would run errands for neighbours to make a penny or two, or they might go round trying to find discarded empty bottles on which the pub might pay back a penny deposit. But one of the best stories of financial opportunism came from another Manchester child. Outside the window of a local sweetshop was a big grating which led down into the coal cellar. Every now and then someone would drop a penny by mistake down into the cellar, where it would lie in full view. If this lad or one of his friends discovered that this had happened, they would go in and ask the shopkeeper, who knew them a little through Sunday school, to get 'their' penny back for them. Their word was never doubted and the shopkeeper's willingness to go and fetch it always secured another day's supply of sweets.

Generally, most adults seem to have been good to the local children. Many bakeries offered bags of broken biscuits to them, perhaps for only a halfpenny or a penny. On New Year's Day the children would go round all the corner shops to wish the owners a happy new year, and would be given an orange or a handful of sweets so long as the shopkeeper knew who they were.

One great delight for many children was the weekly or monthly comic. Titles like the *Skipper* and the *Tiger*, now long gone, were the chief form of escapism for 1920s boys. And for the more sophisticated there was *Rainbow*, a more factual magazine for those who wanted to broaden their horizons, or more likely rather for those whose parents wanted them to broaden their horizons. Because cash was limited there was a great network of comic-swapping in each district. Little boys would turn up on each other's doorsteps clutching a bundle of already finished comics to exchange for ones not yet read.

Shortage of cash also meant that toys were few and far between and most children had to improvise. Small girls would hunt for pieces of broken pot with a patch of silver or gold paint on them and then, using them as 'shillings', play shops happily for hours on the back steps, often with many of the less breakable knickknacks from around the house. Other popular games cost just as little to play: hopscotch was a favourite, as was skipping with pieces of old rope. Rope could also make a passable swing if attached to a lamppost, and the policeman wasn't about.

In many places there was ready-made entertainment. In East London in particular, there were frequent visits by barrel organ grinders, with the obligatory monkey. Sometimes there were other street entertainers, or visits from the muffin man or the Welsh cockle girl, singing away, although these did need more money. A girl who was at elementary school in Bristol remembers that her singing class often used to take its note from the cockle girl as she traded her wares outside.

If you were lucky there might be a park a few tram stops away, and on occasions a group of children might be allowed to spend an afternoon there, perhaps with a bag of sand-wiches and a bottle of water: untold delight. Indeed, the arrival of the tram at the turn of the century had transformed the life of most slum dwellers. Now the edge of town, and hence the countryside, was only a tram ride away, and every now and then the whole family might take a trip out there. A quarter of a century earlier few children, or adults for that matter, had ever seen rolling green fields, cows or sheep. And even in the twenties this was sometimes true. A young priest from the Potteries once took a group of Sunday school children on a trip to the country. Many of the children had no idea what a cow or a sheep even looked like.

The other main activity for many children outside school hours was one already mentioned, the Sunday school. Apart from the social side of the schools, both for children and adults, those young people who attended on a Sunday were given the opportunity to broaden their education over and above the rather rudimentary teaching provided at the elementary schools. Furthermore, for those who wished to rise up the social scale, perhaps to become managers in factories or to become teachers, the Sunday schools provided this extra educational opportunity and also brought them into direct contact with a class of people well above their own. Most Sunday schools had considerable middle-class involvement, chiefly because all classes went to church, and, nominally at least, the Sunday schools were an extension of the churches. Furthermore, they provided an ideal vehicle for the wealthier classes to become involved in the community. Although, at school, richer and poorer kids mixed freely together, a young person from a humble background would have little contact with middle class adults, except in the future with employers. In the Sunday schools this was less true, and it gave intelligent, aspiring working-class young people the chance to become more educated — and more importantly, the chance to be noticed. Sometimes this provided vital opportunities for self-advancement.

Furthermore, Sunday schools gave many young people their first opportunity to hold any degree of responsibility. As they grew older there were opportunities for organisation, perhaps of social events, or of one-off lectures to classes in the school. Some of the most promising pupils in their mid-to-late teens even became Sunday school teachers — mainly of the younger children, but even so it gave them a rare chance positively to demonstrate their abilities and gain invaluable experience.

The point was that even if a child was extremely talented, financial necessity often meant the mill or the mine was the only option when he or she left school. Parents who had received little education, and who had no ambition for their children, saw no reason for there to be any alternative. What the Sunday school did was bring the young working-class person into contact with an employer class both able to offer advice and possibly a job with prospects. Typical was the son of a working-class family who, through his contacts with the church and the Sunday school, was offered a job as a clerk by a local brewer. He ended up as one of the brewery managers. Often young people secured jobs as school-teachers through the Sunday school or through church. The employers were the governors, and the teachers and school heads were often pillars of the local church establishment. If a young pupil shone in front of them at Sunday school, then opportunity might appear for the future. In the end it came down to the old adage — it isn't what you do, it's who you know. Sunday school gave a working-class child the chance to meet people who could provide opportunities in life, and many found it to be their escape route from the slums.

The emphasis in Sunday schools was very much upon self-improvement. Some schools sponsored missionaries, and children were urged to raise as much money to fund their work. Often there would be an incentive to do so, and almost invariably a reward of an educational nature, most probably a book voucher. Musical and dramatic activities not only provided entertainment for all connected with the school, but also broadened the literary horizons of those involved with them.

The principal time when the school met was on a Sunday afternoon, and a book prize was awarded to the best attenders at the end of the year. Classes were divided according to age group. In the primary department teaching tended to be solely religious, with children learning and reading from cards with biblical texts upon them. Though there was a strong emphasis upon religious teaching right the way through the school, as children grew older the scope of their education was broadened, perhaps with musical and literary classes, or lectures from visiting speakers on a wide range of topics.

But the Sunday school was not by any means all work for the young. There were annual Christmas parties in the various departments; in the primary department of one school, for example, every child had to do a little act in a show for the rest. There was the annual outing when huge parties of children and young people piled into a train and went off into the countryside with a vast picnic, often to a place of historical interest where the young could play and the older could explore. In many homes the Sunday school annual outing was one of the most important events of the year — perhaps the excuse for the children to have a new pair of shoes or a new set of clothes.

The majority of working-class chidren in the years after the War found themselves in a vicious circle. The experience of a young man from Bolton, who left school just after the end of the War, was typical: he left school at lunchtime one day, aged fourteen. The same afternoon his mother took him down to the local colliery to see if there was work for him 'down t'pit'. There wasn't, but there was at the next place she tried, a cotton mill just up the road. And so he ended up working in the mill. It was as simple as that. No question of choice: his mother just wanted to find him a job. There was no particular selfishness in this, it was just that the majority of working-class adults had no higher perceptions. They simply didn't think of working anywhere but the local mill, pit or factory. And fourteen-year-old children had no real say in the matter.

Furthermore, many parents in the early twenties saw it as their right to push their children into paid employment at the first possible opportunity to bring some extra income into the home. After slaving for years to feed and clothe their families, many fathers saw it as only fair for them to see a little return now the children were older. And though the War had mellowed many fathers, they were still very much the head of the household. If they wanted children to work, not learn, or to remain at home helping their mothers, there was little opportunity for argument.

Where there was dissent, friction was inevitable. One Yorkshire girl left school and worked in the mill for a while on her father's orders. But she hated it, and set herself the task of escaping into clerical work. After much effort, learning typing and shorthand at night school, she secured a job in a shipping office, but at a reduced wage. That caused enough trouble in itself, but when she also decided to become independent and set herself up in her own room away from home, she literally had to run away. Though she saw her mother often afterwards, her father never had anything to do with her again: he had been deprived of his rights.

Few children dared to do the same. Most went out to serve their apprenticeships, and brought home perhaps fifteen shillings or a pound a week for their mothers. Of this they might be given back perhaps a shilling as pocket money. Yet this was never really questioned. In those days, to the school leaver, a shilling or two was still a small fortune.

And for those who did try to set themselves up for a better life, it could be a long and difficult struggle to do so. Another girl from a Yorkshire mill community resolved to become a nurse. She found a junior job in a local hospital, but had to borrow heavily from relatives and friends to pay for her uniform. Most of her earnings once she had started were spent on text books for nursing exams, and for the best part of a year she didn't even go out of the hospital grounds because her shoes leaked and she hadn't the money to replace them. But she was one of the lucky ones. She did well, passed her exams and in later life ended up with her own house and started a nursing home. Few, though, had the determination or good fortune to find and follow such a path.

The only other real way out of the slum existence for the majority of children lay, though, in the very rare chance of either winning a scholarship to the fee-paying grammar schools, or having sufficiently enlightened parents who wished their offspring to get on, and had the means to help them. And at that they still had to be lucky enough and bright enough to pass the exam which gave access to a secondary education.

For many of those working-class children who did get to grammar school, the first day of term was a tremendous culture shock. It was a surprise to many to find that books were now abundant, but had to be paid for. A Manchester boy, who was lucky enough to have parents who skimped and saved to send him to grammar school, was amazed to find that he was about to begin learning foreign languages. In the slums such things were unimaginable. Many children now needed to buy sports equipment although in some places it could be borrowed. To do without would have been impossible, for sport was a very important part of grammar school life. To many parents who had stretched their resources to the limit to pay the fees, this must have been a rude shock.

But the effort was well worthwhile. By comparison with education in the elementary schools, grammar school was a wonderland. Teaching in elementary schools revolved around the 'three Rs', reading, writing and arithmetic. Other subjects, like history and geography were taught, but not in great depth.

But grammar school education was altogether more sophisticated. Literature was introduced into English teaching, with those working-class children who made it to join their middle-class counterparts making their first acquaintance with poetry and the classic novels. More advanced mathematics came into the curriculum, with algebra and arithmetic altogether more sophisticated than that taught in the elementary schools, as well as geometry lessons. In all grammar schools, Latin was a must, and many children learned Greek as well. Apart from the classics, there was French — something barely even contem-

A gargling parade. Influenza was rife in Europe, and many methods were tried to ward off the disease, then a considerable killer. Boys — apparently the school's shooting team — of a Lichfield grammar school in 1919.

plated by those children who made it to the grammar school from the humblest backgrounds. And for the first time there was proper science teaching. Elementary schools did often provide a little science, but it was very basic.

All grammar schools still had regular religious teaching, though the emphasis on religion as part of school curricula had declined over the previous century along with the numbers who attended church on a Sunday. In the early part of the nineteenth century there had been bitter disputes between the Anglican Church and Nonconformists about the doctrine of religious teaching, and as a result the growth of an education system for all had been delayed for years as the two sides wrangled. But by the later part of the century that religious fervour had waned, and the state school system was able to develop free from theological bigotry. By the twenties teaching was factual and not particularly doctrinaire.

The immediate target of the grammar school education was the Matriculation, a set of exams taken around the age of sixteen, and very similar to today's O Levels. For those bright enough there was the Oxford and Cambridge entrance exam as well. But that was really the province of the children of the employer class, the well to do with ambitions and horizons beyond those of the upwardly mobile slum child. Very very few of them ever reached the highest seats of learning.

In many senses the grammar schools were the poor man's public school. They had a very strong corporate spirit. For example, uniform was obligatory there, and it was a near criminal act to be caught without one's cap on. Sport was a very important part of the curriculum. Pupils were expected to follow the success or failure of the various school teams, and at least one northern grammar school the headmaster would question boys at random during morning assembly, and woe betide anyone who did not know the previous day's scores. At most grammar schools at least one whole afternoon each week was spent out on the playing fields, and a number of PT lessons were given during the rest of the week as well. Within the school hierarchy, members of the first eleven or fifteen were held in great esteem. It was a position to which every boy aspired.

Discipline within the school was even more severe than in the elementary school, although respect for teachers was very strong and curbed a lot of mischief. Those who stepped out of line stayed behind at the end of the day on detention, or wrote lines like their public school counterparts. There were often cases, though, when punishment returned to the physical, and sometimes brutally. One old grammar school boy remembers a French teacher with a ferocious temper who once actually beat unconscious a boy who hadn't done his homework. Another teacher would grab boys and hurl them to the floor, regardless of the consequences. Often they were cut badly. Fortunately, however, such occurrences were not all that common.

The effect of a grammar school education on most working-class pupils who made it there was in many ways similar to, but greater than, that achieved by close involvement with the Sunday school. A grammar school pupil not only gained the status of his education, which opened up whole new career vistas, but also came into contact with the parents of more prosperous friends who might themselves become contacts who could help find good opportunities for the future. In the twenties education was a sign of social standing which could secure otherwise unhoped-for advancement, and which conveyed to a young person from the humblest background a certain degree of respectability in society. Unlike most of their childhood friends, those who made it to grammar school found the way out of the slums.

Few were so lucky, though. And fate was often horribly cruel. One Yorkshire girl, about to continue on to a secondary education, saw her dreams evaporate with the sudden death of her father. As the oldest child she had to go into the dreaded mill to keep the rest of her family alive. And for the majority there was no hope of leaving the slums. Perhaps few really even considered doing so. Those narrow streets, the pits and the mills were a way of life. To most people there was no alternative. There they were born, worked, bred and died. Except, perhaps, for the occasional holiday, the world outside was little more than an illusion.

BREAKING OUT

The world to which the soldiers came back, particularly in the towns and cities, may indeed have been very much the same as it had been when they left. In the working-class communities in particular, the way of life was little changed from a quarter of a century earlier. But in 1919 a new mood was afoot in the little streets. The War which had taken so many lives and caused so much anguish was finally over. And, despite the great loss, the people were determined once more to enjoy themselves. One of the strongest surviving images of England in the 1920s is that of the frivolity and gaiety, almost a collective desire to put out of the mind all the horrors that were past. Though the bubble of enthusiasm would soon be burst by the return of harsh economic reality and the growth of unemployment, the new mood did not die out altogether. The collective suffering endured by a generation had changed their attitudes and those of their successors for good.

The fun began as soon as the boys came home. All those who survived came back with a special demobilisation bonus, perhaps as much as forty pounds. There were family celebrations and street parties and every night pubs, cinemas and dance halls were packed to the doors with people enjoying themselves. And the euphoria was not short-lived. For months this continuous merriment was visible everywhere. People wrote letters to *The Times* complaining that morality had gone to the dogs — all this decadence simply wasn't right. The fun was helped by the postwar boom — indeed, in many senses it caused it. Some breweries, for example, worked overtime to keep up with demand in the pubs, and a few even had to work twenty-four hours a day. Money earned in the trenches or the munitions factories flowed freely. But when the economic downturn came in 1920, life for the older generation returned abruptly to reality.

For the younger generation, though still partly fettered by parents and social conditioning, things would never be the same. The most obvious feature of the lives of the young in the years immediately after the War was that many, particularly those who had seen active service, were far less subservient, far less inclined to bow to their elders and betters. Fathers who had been at home for the War found older children, perhaps influenced by workmates or brothers who fought in the War, far less inclined blindly to obey orders or to toe the family line. It would, for example, have been almost incomprehensible for the mill lass mentioned in the previous chapter to think of setting up her own home before the War. Such things just weren't done.

Fathers were astonished — even horrified — to find their own sons standing beside them in the pub. Before 1914 that would have been unheard of. But now young men increasingly spent their leisure time in the pubs. And to make matters worse, women too now began appearing in the lounge bars of these once male sanctuaries. Some, more enlightened men, happily took their wives down with them on a Saturday night and drank in mixed groups. But for the majority that would have been too bitter a draught to swallow.

This reluctance to conform or to be subservient to the higher classes was reflected in changing attitudes to a career in service afer the War. Before 1914 entry into the staff of a middle or upper class home was regarded as a good thing for the teenage daughters of the working class. In 1900 domestic service had been the largest provider of employment in the country. In 1914 some one and a quarter million women still worked in service. Indeed it was the only widespread employment available for most women. But by 1919 it was becoming increasingly difficult to get servants to work in the home. To the shock of the matriarchy, many young girls flatly refused to enter service. Many would accept any kind of job in industry, or in a shop, rather than enter service. The principal reasons for this were twofold. First, there was the simple question of subservience — young people were less inclined to serve. And then there was the problem of the restrictive nature of service, discussed in greater detail in chapter 12. In an age where the young were acquiring unprecedented freedom, there were fewer girls ready to lead the confined, old-fashioned life of the servants' quarters, where fun and games and contact with men were seldom evident.

Perhaps for the first time among the lower classes, personal appearance became important. Boys and girls alike began to take trouble in preparing themselves before going out dancing or to the cinema. Girls in particular became more fashion-conscious than ever before, influenced by magazines, cinema idols, and a generation of more liberated girls who had got away from the routine of home during the War. The latest mode, once very much the preserve of the well-off young lady, now became universal among all classes.

The new fashion for girls made its first appearance in the later years of the War as some of them signed up for the womens' corps in the armed forces. Smartly dressed in their new uniforms, their occasional visits to the slum streets shocked the old-fashioned matriarchy. Young girls simply couldn't dress up like that, cut their hair short and swagger around with an air of self-importance. They should know their place.

By 1922 some of the younger women, too, had begun to bob their hair, and use make-up. Even more shocking, though, was the development of the dress worn by unmarried girls, and particularly the appearance of the short skirt. Away from work they began wearing knee-length skirts, silk stockings and vee-necked blouses. Such openness was unprecedented. Fashion had seldom compelled women to cover themselves up completely, but equally there had never been anything quite so blatant as this.

For a few years after the War the schoolboy look was all the rage. Girls cut their hair short, and acquired a very boyish look, with tightly bound breasts and waists, underneath an almost sack-like dress. One historian at least has tried to assign a deep, psychological significance to this desire to assume some degree of masculinity, resulting from the wartime destruction of the balance of the sexes. In reality, though, it was probably just a fashion, and one which was rapidly replaced by a schoolgirl look.

Even so, the development caused ripples of horror among the older generation. As clothes worn by the young became shorter and brighter in colour, so the eyebrows rose still higher and the tongues in the corner shop wagged still faster. The young men in their double-breasted jackets belonged to a world wholly different from that in which their fathers lived, even though they shared the same conditions of life, still depressingly unchanged in much of industrial England. As unemployment rose and wage levels fell back, so disillusion grew. But in the new, gayer social life of the young, with its laxer standards, there was an escape.

The dance was one of the best means of escape. Dancing became universally popular with all classes, but nowhere more so than with working people. Every Saturday night, and often on other nights as well, the cities' dance halls would be packed with the new, slick young generation. For them jazz was the in music, as outrageous in its day as punk rock or the Beatles in theirs. Boys and girls danced together freely and shamelessly in a way their parents never could have dreamed of. Nor was it only jazz. They waltzed and quick-stepped, and later Charlestoned, though the Charleston was not nearly as popular as posterity would have us believe, really only making its appearance in the mid-twenties.

The other new means of escape was the cinema, coming into its own for the first time, and in the process effectively destroying the old music hall. Though stars like Marie Lloyd continued to sing on into the twenties, they were the performers of yesteryear. The men of the moment were the Charlie Chaplins, Buster Keatons and the zany Keystone Kops, as well as the stars of the silent romances and thrillers which always filled a cinema.

The arrival of the cinema was a revolution in its own right. Never before had there been a form of mass entertainment which could cater for all generations, and for both sexes, which could provide a night out for the whole family together, and which attracted employer and employee alike. One northern man remembers an unfortunate occasion when, after being released from work early to go to night school, the train to take him to school did not arrive, and so he decided to go to the cinema instead. But when the lights went up in the interval, he realised that his employer's wife was sitting right behind him.

The cinema industry boomed after the Great War, as more and more people flocked to see stars, such as the great Charlie Chaplin, in silent films like Gold Rush.

And he duly received a severe reprimand the next morning at work. Such an event could not have happened before 1914.

Of course, even in the cinema there was some degree of social distinction, based very much upon the amount of money you had in your pocket. The wealthier classes sat at the back of the stalls or up in the circle if the cinema was big enough to have one. The young people from the slums, with only a few pence to spend, made do with the seats in the pit, as it was known, at the front right under the screen. If, however, they were accompanying a member of the opposite sex, as lovers did and have always done since, they made their way towards an appropriate back row.

The cinema very quickly established itself as one of the most common and popular leisure pastimes, even though it would be some years before talking pictures would replace the often not particularly talented or attentive organ or piano accompanist at the front of the auditorium. It was not long before some cinemas began the Saturday clubs for younger children which would become enormously successful by the 1930s. Particularly for children from poorer districts, it was unprecedented escapism, and often a source of numerous free sweets from cinema proprietors keen to expand their audiences. The success of the cinema was without doubt a strong influence in the development of the new, more rebellious trends in fashion. Stars of the screen became known to vast numbers of people. The cult of mass popularity as we know it today was born and, as happens today, people — particularly the young — began to imitate their heroes. This was seen both in clothing and the use of facial make-up. The Victorians and Edwardians had scarcely ever put anything on their faces in the way of artificial colouring, and though the practice became common among young girls on leave from wartime duties, the strongest influence in the new trend was

The young still wore Sunday best, but on the Sabbath many went to the park, not to church.

56

without doubt the fact that the film stars wore make-up. It is also very probable that the growing concern with one's own appearance stemmed in part from the elegance of some (though not all — Charlie Chaplin scarcely was) of the screen stars.

The cinema was also instrumental in transforming another tradition of working-class life, the Sunday. It was not that people ceased to dress up on a Sunday as they had always done, but rather that for the young there was now something to do other than spend morning and evening in church. For a hundred years congregations had been gradually diminishing, but they were still large in the twenties. But from then on they fell away much more rapidly than before, and this must be attributed at least in part to the fact that there were now other things to do.

Of course, the cinema did not wholly destroy other forms of entertainment. The music hall did survive, even though its heyday was well past. Theatres were popular with many, from all classes. Although often more expensive than the cinema, you could still get threepenny seats on wooden benches at the front of the theatre. Particularly for those working class people who were well read or regularly involved in Sunday schools, the theatre was a very enjoyable way of passing leisure time.

For a young couple or a group of friends a visit to the theatre or cinema would often be coupled with a rare meal out, or perhaps a visit to a cake stall or some similar place on the way there or back. In Birmingham one great favourite was apparently to have a huge mug of hot chocolate and a plate of beans for a shilling before a cinema or theatre trip, and in the East End of London a few pence could buy an enormous slab of cheesecake for those waiting outside cinemas. Cinema queues were often places of great entertainment in themselves, with street artists and amateur comics who would wander up and down the line cracking jokes.

But above all the cinema was a new, and far more accessible, form of escapism for the younger generation of the urban working class in particular, a means of finding a refuge from both the traditional conservatism of slum life, and from the increasing difficulties caused by growing unemployment and economic troubles in the twenties. For a family or married couple, it eclipsed going to church and, to a lesser extent, the pub.

The changing atmosphere and leisure possibilities of the twenties also did much to change the life of young lovers. Before the War the slums were thoroughly unconducive to love, and attitudes within them even more so. Boy-girl relationships were not encouraged, largely because of common anxieties among parents about the danger of losing wage-earning children too soon. Early marriage robbed them of their just rewards for the years of keeping their offspring. As a result, parents often banned their children from going out to dance halls and other popular places of entertainment. It was impossible, too, for young lovers to visit each other at home and obtain any degree of privacy. Even visits with some hope of privacy were often difficult in the cramped conditions of the slum houses. Instead, couples were forced to seek refuge in the narrow alleyways and doorways of slum streets, and in wandering around together. Even this was not always easy. In Salford, for example, one local warehouse owner with strong moral views kept all the recesses around his premises which might be used by courting couples smeared with sticky tar.

By the twenties, however, the lot of young lovers was a much happier one. Parents remained strict, demanding that children should be back by a certain hour, or else all hell would break loose; that much did not change. But there were fewer other constraints. The older generation might not approve of the dance halls, but there was little they could do about it. The back of the cinema provided the opportunity for a little privacy that might not be found elsewhere. It was also easier for young people to go off into any nearby countryside together, or to walk by the river or canal. People tended to go further afield. Sunday night was the great night for courting couples, and any popular walk would be jammed with boys and girls out together.

There was nothing actually new in this. What *was* changing was both the number and the youthfulness of those out walking together. Parents were not amused, but there was little they could really do. When it came down to it, their dominance of children was based upon fear. By the twenties, though father was still very much the boss, children were far more prepared to stand up to him than before.

But one of the most popular images of the twenties, that of far laxer sexual morality, was certainly less true among the working classes than is popularly supposed. Although, in some middle- and upper-class circles there was without doubt a great degree of promiscuity, it is a myth to think that this was the case for the whole of society. The young couples out walking together were freer than ever before, but few took that freedom to the limit before reaching the altar.

Perhaps one reason for this image was the legacy of the War. In all classes there was an element of 'He may never come back, so why should we wait?' In the slum communities some women had become almost amateur prostitutes when the soldiers came home on leave, but at the end of the War they had little status in the community, and were generally treated with hostility.

Nonetheless, there was to some degree an increase in sexual activity in the industrial areas, and indeed throughout society, simply because of improving methods of contraception, and generally increased knowledge about their use. It was the much improved effectiveness of the sheath which made the difference. There had been artificial methods to avoid conception since the 1820s, but amongst the working classes, of whom many were illiterate, very few people knew of their existence. Over the course of the nineteenth century this gradually changed, but even so, in the early years of this century such methods were rarely used. Amongst the majority of working people coitus interruptus was the most popular method of contraception, though some still tried other home-made methods. An oiled sponge, attached with tape, was one frequently used by women, as was the home-made pessary, a mixture of lard and flour.

It was the War which brought widespread contraception to working-class areas. By 1917, despite the best efforts of men like Kitchener to prevent it by urging morality upon his troops, some 20 per cent of the forces in France had contracted venereal disease, and the rate of illegitimate births both there and back in England was reaching an alarming level. In that year the army began to issue sheaths to all serving men. Furthermore, this necessitated something which few working-class men had ever had: actual instruction in contraceptive methods. Previously, sheaths had been dealt with very furtively in the slums, and were little known. The War rapidly ended that.

This was a very important breakthrough. It changed the attitudes of young men dramatically, and brought sexuality much more into the open. Now sexuality was not something which had to be stifled. If a young man wanted to, he had the means to make sure that she couldn't become pregnant. The more daring could now get away with it, even though the majority did not attempt to do so.

Men also became more conscious of sexuality in their relations with each other. Suddenly, sexual prowess, or even access to sheaths and possibly to sexual experience, became an open sign of virility in the pubs and in the workplace. After the end of the War every factory or bar room group had its ex-soldiers, back from the trenches with the new knowledge, and perhaps with a packet of sheaths in their pocket to show off to younger workmates as a sign of manhood. And, of course, experiences with women during the War were related to workmates, providing the generation too young to have fought with a sex education that it would never otherwise have received. The older men might complain about the coarseness of the young, but they secretly enjoyed the openness of their sexual talk. An old barrier had broken down.

Another major breakthrough came with increasing talk and knowledge of sexuality among women as well. Possibly the greatest cause of this was the publication in 1919 of Dr Marie Stopes's book *Married Love*, and Dr Stopes's subsequently unsuccessful libel action against a Catholic critic in 1923, which gave national publicity to contraception. *Married Love* sold in enormous numbers during the twenties and without doubt greatly increased sexual knowledge both inside and outside marriage.

But, despite this vast expansion in sexual knowledge among all classes, and particularly among the lower classes, moral standards simply did not collapse after 1918. Many servicemen with wives back home openly boasted of their fidelity, whether this sprang from genuine feeling, or through lack of success in finding a woman once away, or the fear of contracting venereal disease. The conservatism of the slum streets did not just die when the War ended, though its rigidity began to crack. The wagging tongues of the street could still stigmatise, and in the closeness of the communities little went unnoticed. The other obstacle to sexual laxity was geographical. For the unmarried couple with no access to a bedchamber, there was little opportunity to begin a sexual relationship. Perhaps this, as much as anything, kept up the moral standards of the nation.

Dr Marie Stopes, the architect of birth control and author of Married Love — *the book which did much to increase sexual understanding among the working classes.*

For a generation of girls seeking succour in a relationship with a member of the opposite sex, though, the ghosts of Flanders were ever present. The flower of English youth was dead and in all classes eligible young men were everywhere in short supply. Even today that effect is still visible. Still you can find many octogenarian 'misses'. In some cases of course they are single through choice, but for many there is an old box, full of faded love letters and memories of a youth spoilt by the realities of war. Nowhere was this more true than in the dance halls in England's towns and cities. There every available man had a partner, or could have one if he chose. But around the walls of every hall were large groups of girls, far outnumbering the available men, gathered together waiting, often in vain, for a dancing partner or perhaps something more than that. For many the wait would never end.

Naturally, the result of this was a highly competitive marriage market. The daughters of artisans who once would have barely deigned to mix with the son of a labourer were now only too keen to find a man to love and marry: his background became an irrelevance. Many girls even adapted their personalities just to suit the wishes and needs of the men they picked up. If he was a quiet reserved type, perhaps he might want a kind, homely wife. Or perhaps he was looking for someone more daring and flirtatious. Either way, girls were happy to meet the needs of the available man. Inevitably some, though not many, went to the limit, and in the freer climate of relations between the sexes, tried to win their men through deliberate pregnancy. Those who dared all sometimes failed, but all too often social pressure succeeded in snaring the man in question.

It would, of course, be completely wrong to try to ascribe these changes to the whole of the young postwar generation. Women weren't suddenly transformed into devious and scheming creatures, intent on dragging any man to the altar. But as young people they were freer than ever before, and many women who sought friendship and romance with the opposite sex discovered the numerical reality of the rows of graves on Flanders fields. Nor were they promiscuous in the same way that later generations would be. But by comparison with their parents' generation, brought up at the end of the puritanical Victorian era, when sex really was a dirty word, they were very liberated. In that era the sexuality of the young had been repressed. After 1918 it broke free.

It was not just among the young though that changes were afoot in England's industrial communities. Within the old street communities some of the old values and ties began to disappear. As expectations rose with improved living standards, so people's ethics began to change. Before the War corner shop customers who bought their goods on tick were mostly scrupulously honest even though it was hard to make ends meet and the average working man's wage did not provide for a good and wholesome diet. Now, previously excellent customers began to leave bills unpaid for weeks on end to allow extra spending money. Others tried to falsify their tick books. Many began to live hopelessly beyond their means, buying luxuries unheard of before 1914, eating best butter, salmon, boiled hams, all of which they really couldn't afford. Perhaps the War had relaxed the rigidity of the way of life which always paid the tick at the end of the week, come hell or high water. People just didn't care so much nowadays.

Perhaps inevitably, as the economic prosperity of the months after the end of the War disappeared with the onset of a new decade, and the higher real wage levels were cut back by hard-pressed employers, there was a sharp increase in the crime rate. This was particularly true among the more respectable parts of the working class, something previously unknown. Almost certainly this was due to the conflict between raised expectations and the onset of economic depression. Wages no longer bought the lifestyle enjoyed by many during the postwar boom, but some were unable or unwilling to accept this, and turned to crime as an alternative source of income. Some contemporaries also suggested that a further reason for the trend was the military training that many men had received during the War. Hitherto illiterate or unskilled men now had a far greater degree of technical knowledge than previously, and were better able to master the techniques of robbery. This was particularly true of motor theft and garage break-ins. Men who once had no idea about motor vehicles had been given new knowledge in the army: the car was no longer an alien entity.

Within the working classes the economic downturn of the 1920s helped to break down many of the social barriers which had existed before 1914. Growing unemployment affected all, from the most talented artisan to the most incompetent labourer. People once poles apart in lower-class society now found themselves sharing queues at the dole office. Under these circumstances snobbery could not prevail. Of course this fact must also be qualified, for even at times of record unemployment there is still the majority of the population at work, earning and living unchanging lives. Though cracks began to appear, the old communities were far from shattered. There can be no doubt, though, that the narrowing of divides between different parts of the working-class world, coupled with growing intermarriage between families which would previously have had little or no contact, was instrumental in raising many young men from humble backgrounds up the social scale. With this came a growing appetite for self-improvement among the young. Many began attending night school and part-time courses at technical colleges, and reading became far more popular as a pastime than ever before. For the first time working men could be found in increasingly large numbers in local public libraries. It was a comparatively slow change. In Lancashire in 1926, for example, the local library service still had only 8,000 readers and a book list of only about 20,000 volumes, but by the mid-1930s these figures had increased by twenty and fifteen times respectively. The result was an increasingly better-educated working class, made up of men better able and more willing to think for themselves. Old values were more likely to be questioned and, where they made little sense, to be rejected. The power of the street matriarchy to order and damn was gradually eroded away as the years went by and the twenties drew to a close.

Furthermore, the newly enfranchised working class was in a position to make its voice heard, able as it now was to dictate the rise and fall of politicians and governments. With this came an increase in the voice of the politics of the left, and of the trade union movement, discussed in the next chapter.

Not all these changes happened overnight, and the slum way of life was only really broken down by the redevelopment programmes of the 1930s and by the destructive power of Hitler's Luftwaffe. But within the red-brick streets attitudes had changed, particularly among the young, but also among some of their parents' generation. The children of the Edwardian working classes had led regimented and disciplined lives, within both the strict rules of home and school during childhood, and later the constraints of work and marriage. In short, they lived, but few had fun. But after 1918 the breakout began from this rigid lifestyle. It remained hard to avoid going down the pit or working in the mill, and to really escape one's social background. But now, for the young, life became more enjo
their red-brick communities. There was more to look forward to than their parents' generation ever had.

THE GENERAL STRIKE

Though the prime aim of this book is to portray life in the years after the War, rather than the notable events of that period, the General Strike looms so large in our image of the 1920s that it cannot be ignored, even though surprisingly few of my interviewees had any particularly clear memories of it as an event in their lives. Nonetheless, it deserves some mention, if only to explain where it fits into this era. The strike lasted nine days and was really a total disaster for the Labour movement. It was called in support of a strike in the coal industry — in fact the miners were soon abandoned to fight alone for months before being finally forced into submission by economic hardship. And in an era that had witnessed the turbulent events of the Russian Revolution, the failure of the General Strike to cow the Government into submission was ample proof that those who preached a repeat of that revolution in Britain were in for a long wait.

The political mood of the British people was much changed by events during the War. The introduction of one man, one vote, in the 1918 Representation of the People Act was just a symptom of this. Perhaps because the ordinary man had, for the first time, come to be involved with the welfare of his country, or perhaps because of the general sentiment that it should never happen again, men became more politically thoughtful, and their politics more radical. Before the War, most ordinary people had shared a strong sense of class identity but it was limited to their perception of being part of a particular class. It was still us and them, but when election time came round, those who had the vote tended still to follow the lead of the middle and upper classes, who dominated the Liberal and Conservative parties. The Labour Party did make some headway during the Edwardian years, but that headway remained relatively limited.

But by 1918 the working-class man, probably equipped for the first time with a vote, and a small say in his local and national affairs, was thinking differently. The working classes were becoming more politically class conscious, aware that they did have a political party to represent their own interests. And the result was clear to see. Within a decade the Liberal Party, which a generation earlier had vanquished all opposition at the polls, had virtually been eliminated as a political force, eclipsed by the increasing polarisation of politics between the Conservatives — the party, primarily, of the better off — and the Labour movement.

Much of the drift towards Labour and socialism came from the young. Many members of the older generation found talk of socialism, profit, and the capitalist profit unnecessarily subversive. Their generation had talked of trade unionism and the way it would improve the lot of the ordinary man, but without the additional requirement that the rich should be fleeced to pay for it.

Not that, in reality, the growth of support for Labour marked a real move towards extremism in the lower classes. After the Russian Revolution several hundred Marxists had gathered in Leeds to prepare for the inevitable sequel in Britain. There were even Soviets in a number of towns and cities for a time. But they were lone voices. The working classes were not ripe for rebellion, and the pleas of the extremists fell upon deaf ears. In Salford Robert Roberts recalls that there was great interest when a group was set up to study 'the first nine chapters of *Das Kapital*'. Fifty-four people attended the first classes after a fanfare opening in one of the local trade clubs. But it was not long before those fifty-four had dwindled to just three; the working classes were not really interested in the man who was supposed to bring them liberation. Similar efforts were made throughout the country, and most failed absolutely to attract the support their organisers had anticipated.

In fact the Government never quite realised this, and rather overreacted to the appearance of a number of apostles of revolution who toured industrial districts in the postwar years preaching to the proletariat, urging the workers to rise and free themselves of their Marxist chains. The workers themselves were mostly uninterested, but the Government rushed to set up a 'Citizen Guard' of volunteers to resist industrial sabotage through widespread striking. The plan was for members of the public to fill in if services were crippled by militant strikers. There were howls of protest from the unions, and the public, at what was effectively organised strike-breaking, and the idea was soon dropped. It was ironic, though, that precisely these tactics would be used when the crunch finally did come in 1926.

Even so, people were more politically aware than they had been before the War. In those days speakers from left-wing groups who stood up on soap boxes to preach their message were generally ignored. But by the early twenties that had all changed. Instead, a political speaker could quickly attract a large audience and start a long political debate with the crowd. Political journals and books began to attract a much larger working class readership. And a left-wing newspaper, like the growing *Daily Herald*, was guaranteed an increasing level of sales. By the early twenties the *Herald* had a circulation of around 300,000 copies, and a much higher readership than that.

The growth of the Labour movement and of working-class politics after the War was mirrored in a corresponding growth in the trade union movement. Prior to the last years of the Edwardian era, the union movement had remained primarily the domain of the skilled working class, made up of unions of craftsmen rather than labourers. To some extent this situation remained after the end of the fighting in 1918. In the textile industry, for example, the unions were still very much dominated by the skilled workers, although the membership doors had been opened more widely in the previous decade.

But generally, though, union membership was now far more broadly spread than it had been before. This change was reflected in the rapid growth of the movement. In 1920 there were some eight million union members, compared with only around half that amount in the years leading up to the War. The average size of individual unions also rose, from a little over 3,000 to almost 4,500. In other words, not only were there more unionists, but also the size of individual unions, and as a result the power they wielded, was growing as well. It would be surprising if this consideration did not lead many union leaders to somewhat overrate their power and influence in the early twenties.

Interestingly, though many unions were still run by the more skilled members of a particular workforce, overall the proportion of trade union members in the more traditional industries, such as textiles and mining, had actually fallen fairly sharply. Before the First World War some 30 per cent of union members had worked in these industries. By 1926 that figure had fallen to only just over 20 per cent.

The point of all these comparisons is not simply statistical; it in fact shows a change in the balance of views within the trade union movement. The reduction in the percentage of union members in the older industrial sector did not obviously mean that there were fewer men working in that sector, since the lower percentage was of a much higher figure. But the fact remained that increasing numbers of union members no longer came from the older working-class elites, a fact which certainly affected the political tone of the union movement. Socialism was not really the preserve of the old 'labour aristocracy', as it has been nicknamed by some. In many industrial areas, and particularly those where the older industries provided the bulk of the jobs, the more respectable members of the working class actually rather frowned on socialist views and on support for the Labour Party. They continued for many years to vote Liberal, but as that party declined out of political reckoning, so their votes moved towards the Conservatives.

There can be no doubt that the growing move among the working classes towards class politics and support for socialism was a contributing factor to the fact that the first few years after the War saw severe industrial disruption and frequent failures in industrial relations. But, of course, this was far from being the only reason. In fact, the use of large, national strikes as a form of protest was still a relatively new one. Although there had been sporadic major industrial outbreaks during the previous century, it was not until the last few years before 1914 that unions began to use this form of action to some effect and on a regular basis.

Without doubt, though, the economic crisis which came shortly after the end of the War, and which has already been mentioned extensively, was the prime reason for the degree of industrial unrest that there was. The failure of British industry to recover its pre-war markets meant that the high wage levels which had arisen as a result of the conflict could not be maintained by the employers. Hardly surprisingly, the economic necessity to cut wages was not one which workers could readily identify with, and it was the role of the mushrooming union movement to resist those economic pressures.

But not all strikes were purely economic in motive. Even before the end of the War there had been a police strike in London, followed by similar disputes a year later in both London and Liverpool. Each action sought to secure the right to join a union for the police force. In London the strikes were failures, but in Liverpool the reverse was true, and troops had to be called in to keep order and to stamp out troubles which arose as a result of the strike.

There were a number of attempts to secure better industrial relations. The first step after the end of the War was the establishment of what were known as Whitley Councils, made up of both employers and union leaders, which were designed to offer some degree of worker participation in industry. But the attempt was not a great success. The more militant unions refused to accept the idea of cooperation with the bourgeois capitalists, and at local level many managers were reluctant to introduce any such apparatus for fear of it harming their prerogative of managing.

There were also moves to establish negotiating machinery for industry, through the Industrial Courts Act of 1919. The courts were essentially arbitration tribunals, and met with some success, most notably in the settlement of a dock strike the following year.

But nonetheless these were turbulent times for the industrial sector. During the econ-

A.J. Cook, the miners' leader who led the dispute which caused the 1926 General Strike, here speaking at the 57th annual gala day of the Northumberland miners, 1929.

omic troubles of the early twenties there were major industrial disputes on the railways and among the transport workers. But the worst conflict was to come in the mines, and it was this which would cause the 1926 turmoil and Britain's first and only real General Strike.

The troubles began in 1921. In that year the Government announced that it was to return the mines to private ownership — they had been under state control since early on in the War — and met with outright hostility from the unions, which feared that the mine owners would seek lower wage levels to improve competitiveness. Negotiations between all sides failed, and on the date set for the return of control the men came out. But the miners were let down by their traditional allies in industrial politics — the railwaymen and the transport workers — and the strike broke down after two months of bitter conflict. Wage reductions were imposed on the miners, but Parliament also passed a bill which limited the working day in the pits to seven hours. Four years later that step would make itself very much felt in discussions over the future of the industry.

Between 1922 and 1924 the economy took a turn for the better. Profits rose, unemployment ceased its upward trend, and labour relations took a dramatic turn for the better. Morale in the labour movement was raised further by the party's successes at the polls in 1924. There was jubilation in the slum streets on the night of victory, and the young socialists and union activists thought it the dawning of a new age. It was not to be. Ramsay MacDonald's government was both inexperienced and, more importantly, without a majority in the House of Commons, dependent on the Liberals to pass legislation.

Furthermore, once in power, the Labour leadership acted much like any other. It had not the power to make radical changes, and so, once in power, had to act for the needs of the country as best it could. Inevitably this sometimes brought conflict with the unrealistic demands from some in the movement and the class that government had been elected to represent. In that year there were short-lived strikes in both the docks and on the London trams. Both were quickly settled but not before emergency plans had been drawn up to provide alternative services for the ordinary people to replace those lost as a result of the strikes. For the union leaders it was a dilemma. The future cabinet minister Ernest Bevin, who was then leader of the dockers, commented at the time about the extraordinary difficulty of operating under a Labour government. One could fight the Tories and resist their threats: it was less easy when the opponents were supposed to be on your side.

This difficulty, and the eclipse of Labour and the Liberals in the 1924 General Election, restored a sense of militancy to the union leaders, who were now more prepared than ever to use the industrial weapon. They could see no alternative.

Trouble in the coal industry resurfaced in 1925 when employers, who a year earlier had granted a particularly generous wage settlement, tried to restore lower wage levels and increase the working day in the face of tumbling profits. The miners were unimpressed, but because of high coal stocks were reluctant to take industrial action without the backing of other unions that had been denied them four years earlier. This time they were more fortunate: the TUC General Council offered its support, and the railwaymen and transport workers agreed to black the movement of coal. But at this point the Government intervened and offered a temporary subsidy to the industry while a Royal Commission tried to sort out its problems.

For a few months peace reigned, but when the Commission reported early in 1926 it recommended some reduction in wages as essential to making the industry profitable. The miners refused to accept its findings, and prepared for industrial action. At the same time the TUC held a special conference which pledged support for the miners. Last-minute negotiations with the Government failed, and on 4 May the so-called General Strike began.

In fact, the term 'general' for the strike is not entirely accurate. Apart from the one million miners who came out, some one and a half million others struck in support. The TUC did allow some workers to continue, particularly in the postal service and in textiles; engineers and shipbuilders were only called out after a week. But in those areas which were selected for action the response was total. Less than 1 per cent of railwaymen worked, trams and buses ground to a halt, and power stations and the docks were both closed. The national press was also removed from the streets.

But ever since the TUC had first voiced its support for the miners' cause in the previous year, the Government had been preparing itself for the possibility of a major industrial outbreak of this kind, and when the Strike came contingency plans were ready to be put straight into action.

At first troops, police and special constables were used to keep essential supplies going. Then large numbers of volunteers were recruited to get the transport system going again. There were no shortages of would-be train drivers and bus conductors, particularly from among the students of Oxford and Cambridge, who abandoned their studies and swarmed throughout the country taking over the strikers' work, and often leaving chaos in their wake. Getting a few buses on the road, and sorting out the unloading of ships in the ports was one thing, actually using volunteers to run the railways was another altogether. One lady remembers returning from the Continent during the Strike and boarding a train at Dover. But at the time of departure, the train, guided by undergraduate hands, actually moved out of the station backwards and in the direction of the Channel from where most of the passengers had just come. Other incidents were less amusing: the carelessness of a

During the General Strike, volunteers were recruited to drive buses and trains in order to keep the transport system going. They were vilified, and sometimes attacked, by those supporting the Strike.

student signalman in East Anglia in letting two trains into the same section of the track led to a serious crash in which there was at least one death and a number of injuries. The student network was also hopelessly inefficient, with few services running to anything like the normal schedule. In fact on of the local strike committees organised by the trade union movement put out a rather sarcastic notice suggesting that the new railway regime was to introduce luncheon cars on trains between Westminster and Blackfriars in London.

Relations between strikers and strike breakers varied. There were frequent missile attacks on buses and trains being driven by the blackleg labour, and in Newcastle there was rioting, baton charges by the police and arrests of strike leaders. By contrast, in Plymouth relations were sufficiently cordial that a football match was held between the strikers and the local police.

As the Strike continued the union leaders found themselves in an increasingly difficult position. Their dilemma was, quite simply, that the Strike was, in their eyes if not in those of many of their supporters, intended to achieve industrial ends. It was not meant to be a revolution. Indeed they were as much afraid of a state of political chaos as the Government was. Furthermore, the Government's preparation for confrontation was clearly being seen to work. Supplies were getting through, albeit haphazardly, and the Strike had attracted relatively little widespread support outside the mainstream union movement. As has been so often the case in modern history, the strongest political force remained that of apathy.

For the moderate members of the TUC's General Council it was obvious that since they were not seeking revolution, some form of negotiation would have to take place. Furthermore, many of them were afraid of the forces they had unleashed, and had doubts about how long they could remain in control of the situation.

The result was rapid and very definite backtracking by the TUC. Herbert Samuel, the

Food convoys during the Strike were given military protection to make sure that strikers did not stop them from getting through. The Army also took over many essential services, as well as helping to control the strikers.

man who had chaired the 1925 Royal Commission, put together a number of proposals to solve the miners' dispute, which were rejected by the miners themselves but accepted by the TUC negotiating committee. In reality the TUC leaders had decided upon a complete surrender, and in that decision the miners and their troubles were conveniently put to one side. The union chiefs had started something they felt unable to control, and took the first opportunity presented to them to back out. After only nine days the order to return to work was issued to the country. The miners were abandoned to fight alone, which they duly did, until the autumn when poverty and desperation finally drove them into submission.

The more militant, left-wing members of the Labour movement were quick to accuse their leaders of betrayal. But the reality was less clearcut. The England left after 1918, the land fit for heroes that never quite was, was ready for increased political consciousness amongst the lower classes, strengthened by the extension of the suffrage and the War years that had shown just how fragile the social divide could be.

But what nobody really knew was in what way that growth of consciousness could be directed. Britain in the 1920s was not ripe for revolution as Russia had been in 1917, and most Labour and union leaders well realised that. But in 1926 the TUC discovered, to its cost, just how difficult it was to separate industrial and political ambitions. Realising that difficulty, they backed down rapidly before a situation could arise which might bring political troubles on a scale that none of them wanted.

The new age that the young socialists had acclaimed on the night of electoral triumph in 1924 was still some way off. After 1926 the union movement was somewhat discredited, and the sharp rise in membership over the previous few years was suddenly reversed. Although there would be one more Labour government later in the decade, it would not be until after another war that socialist policies, carefully thought out and with popular support, would make their mark. 1926 showed the Labour movement that this was the only road it could take. The path to revolution was an impassable one. As the famous Labour writer Beatrice Webb wrote in her diary when the strike was over, its failure had shown just what a sane people the British really are.

Country Life

IN ENGLAND'S GREEN AND PLEASANT LAND

There is no doubt that there is a certain nostalgia in these days of widespread factory farming for the days when England's green and pleasant land was just that. Instead of barbed wire and motorways, of single fields which encompass areas where once there might have been three or four pretty meadows, of bare areas where once long rows of elms stood, there were small fields broken up by green hedgerows and occasional copses. In the more rugged areas of the north and west country, the stone walls which walkers now clamber over with little regard for their stability still served as vital fencing for the moorland cottages and farms to be found dotted all across the countryside, and which are now mostly ruined. It was still the England of the smallholding. Today farming is mostly the prerogative of the large farmer.

The years after the First World War were years of crisis for the countryside, for economic reasons and because of the sharp rise in the importance of manufacturing over the previous century which had caused a decline in the importance of agriculture. The result of that had been a steady flow of people out of the countryside in search of new opportunities in the towns and cities. Where once sons had always followed in their fathers' footsteps, many chose now to make their lives elsewhere.

The farms themselves, though, changed very little in these years, at any rate in terms of size and type. As will be seen in the later chapter on ancestral estates, there was a huge transition in land ownership after the First World War, on a scale unparalleled since the Norman Conquest. All over the country landowners moved their wealth out of their estates and into bonds, stocks and shares. In practical terms, though, the impact on the individual farms was minimal. While some landowners sold out their holdings in bulk, the majority of the new purchasers were the tenants who already farmed their own particular parcel of the estates. They took out mortgages and bought their own farms.

In the buoyancy of the postwar boom this shift in ownership to the former tenant farmers looked promising for those who participated. Until the early twenties the market for farm produce was good, and there was every reason to look forward to a prosperous future. But those aspirations were to be dashed when economic depression returned in 1920 and 1921. At that point farmers began to find themselves heavily burdened by those same mortgages that had seemed so painless only a year or two earlier. And whilst other parts of the economy saw some periods of prosperity throughout the decade, agriculture was destined to remain depressed throughout the 1920s.

73

As the world economy returned to normal after the end of the First World War, it rapidly became evident that there was a world surplus of many primary products — basic raw materials, agricultural produce and so forth. In the agricultural sector farmers saw the price at which they could sell cereal crops, for example, fall steadily over the course of the following decade or so, making it difficult or actually impossible for an arable farmer to make a living, particularly if he had bought his farm. The result was that many farmers switched to dairy farming, which didn't suffer as greatly from world over-capacity. Ironically, though, so many farmers switched to dairy farming during the 1920s that by the beginning of the next decade there was a glut of dairy products in Britain, which was only eased by the creation of the Milk Marketing Board and the beginning of the promotion of milk as essential to health.

But the widespread switch to dairy from arable farming did not quite cure the depression in agriculture. Falling profits reduced wage levels from an average of 40 shillings a week after the War to only 25 shillings by 1923. In that year labourers in Norfolk went on strike to prevent wages dropping even lower and, although they won, not all of those who stopped work found their old jobs there when they tried to return. It was a lesson learned elsewhere — there was no strike action in any other part of the country. All in all it was not a good decade for those down on the farm.

After the First World War the countryside remained strangely isolated from the rest of what was a highly industrialised country with very good inter-city and international communications. Country communities were still very insular — there were plenty of members of the older generation who had never really been to a large town, unless there happened to be one nearby. Country folk tended to marry each other and almost everyone had dozens of relatives in their neighbourhood.

Roads in the English countryside remained largely unmade until well into the 1920s and 1930s. Until then, many were just rough tracks, often very dusty, like this lane leading to Kipling's house, Batemans, in Burwash, Sussex.

Roads in much of the English countryside remained largely unmade well into the 1920s and 1930s. Before then they were rough tracks, often with a flint surface, and tended to be very dusty. In one Sussex village only one man actually owned his own car in the early twenties, and one of the other villagers recalled that one could always tell when he was coming, from the enormous dust cloud that rose behind the car as he drove along.

Before made-up roads and motor vehicles became common horses and carts were the only real means of travel between villages, and in the immediate vicinity of each village the majority of people simply walked. The countryside was full of footpaths and shortcuts which could be taken, and travel on foot was very often by far the quickest way of getting somewhere. A five- or six-mile walk was regarded as perfectly normal.

As a result, railway connections were of paramount importance for the farming communities. With motor traffic only just beginning to appear on the roads, trains provided the only easy way for dairy farmers in particular to get their produce to the markets in the towns and cities. It was normal for there to be a daily milk train, for example, from a particular district each day, to which all the local farmers would bring their daily output. Often in a country area this train doubled as the only commuter train from where college students, such as there were, might get into town to study, or where the occasional rural dweller who had a job in town would go to get to work.

But, as was happening in the towns, the gradual increase in the number of motor vehicles in the countryside and the introduction of some mechanised farm machinery had already started to herald the end of the era of horse power on English farms. It was a gradual change — horses were certainly still being used during the Second World War — but there were, by then, few still to be seen on country roads.

Between the wars, most of the farmer's motive power was still provided by horses, and most agricultural equipment — here a harrow — was still horse-drawn.

The general lack of mechanisation was, though, still almost universally reflected in life on the farms. Of course, every farm was better equipped and more efficient than it had been a century earlier, but agriculture remained very much more labour intensive than it is today. Most of the farmer's motive power was also provided by the horse, often by the great shire horses which only really survive today for exhibitive reasons. They pulled ploughs at one end of the year and haycarts at the other, and did much of the work between times besides.

On the dairy farms, naturally, the horse was less important, but the work was no less arduous, and the brunt was borne by the men who milked, fed and tended the livestock. The cows had to be milked twice a day, and often the women of the farm either did all or some of the work involved. And it really was just a matter of a pail, a stool and a pair of hands. It was not until the 1930s that any form of milking equipment came into quite common use, though people had been trying to invent something to do this job for many years. There were some gestures towards hygiene: the bucket into which the milk was put was fitted with a lid to stop dirt getting in when it was being moved around. But basically the milk was just poured straight from the bucket into a churn from which it was sold directly without being treated.

Farming was very much more personalised then than it is today in our age of production quotas and mechanisation. Each man played an important role in his own right, perhaps because of an individual skill. Many of those skills which made men very much a part of the farm have now been superseded by machines. Livestock are now very much just numbers on a list, whereas in the twenties each cow still had a name, and would respond to it.

Since artificial fertilisers to stimulate crop growth were essentially unknown, almost every farm saved manure whenever possible to spread on the fields at a later date. Normally, this was gathered by the cowmen from the sheds during the winter and put into what was known as a midden, which on a large farm could hold several hundred tons of manure. The manure was normally left to rot for around nine months, during which time it had to be turned at least three times. At the end of that time it was loaded into carts and deposited in piles at regular intervals around the fields before being spread around, often by casual labourers working on piecework.

It was not until significantly later that agricultural land began to be drained by networks of underground piping. In the twenties methods were altogether more primitive. One of the most common of these was what was known as 'Bush draining'. This entailed making faggots out of thorn and laying them across channels dug across fields. Earth could then be put back onto the surface, creating a channel down which rainwater could soak away.

Usually, farmers were unable to make their land anywhere like as productive as that same land would be today, not because of improved crop quality or better fertilisers, but because it was logistically impossible to produce as much with old-style farm equipment. Unless the farmer was particularly rich it simply was not possible to employ enough men to harvest, plough and resow crops in the space of time that modern machinery would take. Whilst a field today might produce two, or even sometimes three, crops a year, such productivity was virtually unknown in the twenties.

This is probably one of the key reasons for the dramatic about-turn in the prosperity of country life over the last half-century or so. In the years immediately after 1918 productivity simply was not high enough. In that era of more primitive farming methods and machinery, the seasons were very much more pronounced and important than is now the case. This was not simply a matter of the weather, but rather a kind of calendar for work on the land.

Because of the high labour cost of producing more than one, or possibly two, crops each year on the same piece of land, very few farmers bothered to try to grow a winter crop such as winter corn in the pre-mechanised era, with the result that there was little work in arable areas before spring came and the preparation and sowing of land began. So the coming of spring was awaited eagerly by everybody. Furthermore, the coming of the warmer season was a welcome break from the cold of winter, which in houses and cottages lacking any heating bar an open fire could be extremely uncomfortable.

The last few weeks of the winter were usually devoted to one's own small garden, to preparing it as best one could for the new season so that there was as little work as possible left outstanding once the real work on the farms began. Symbols of the arrival of spring, such as the return of the swallows or the first sound of a cuckoo were watched for with particular attention, and became the talking point of the villages.

The arrival of the spring meant long hours and hard work with such tasks as preparing seed and sowing it, repairing and renewing fencing so that the livestock could be put out to graze on the new year's grass. As soon as that was done on the dairy farms, and the grass was ready for the cattle, the cowmen became semi-redundant, since much of their work, apart from milking, had consisted of mucking out cowsheds and feeding cattle during the winter months when they were inside.

The harvest still looked much like a scene from *Cider With Rosie*, with the entire local community turning out to help gather in the crops. Although not by any means the labour-intensive operation it had been during the nineteenth century, when men with scythes cut entire fields of corn, hay or wheat, the harvest was far from being completely mechanised. Most farms had horsedrawn self-binders, the most complex piece of horse-drawn equipment available to most farmers. It was a machine which cut the crop and threw it out behind tied in sheaves. But most of the rest of the harvest of cereal crops was done by hand, or with relatively primitive hand-powered machinery. Combine harvesters didn't make their first appearance on English farms until the 1930s.

Hay was cut with horsedrawn machinery, but it was turned and gathered by hand and everyone was there to help load it onto huge carts to be taken away for storage. Even schoolchildren rushed home from school to get out into the fields where their parents had been working all day. Some even skipped classes altogether to help. Picking fruit and gathering in root crops was every bit as labour-intensive although, unlike cereal harvesting, methods remain much the same even today.

Every village had its harvest festival when all the local crops had been safely gathered in. The entire community gathered, first in church to give thanks to the Almighty for another year's bread, and then at a local party with a large dinner, plenty of beer and cider, and dancing far into the night.

Away from the farms there was considerable activity in the woodlands, both in pure forestry and timber work, and also in more specialised fields. Most common among these was hoop making from small saplings. Large areas of woodland were never allowed to grow to maturity, and were cut every nine or ten years. The wood produced was made into hoops for barrel making or for holding together packing cases. Some of the saplings were also carved into walking sticks. All the surplus pieces from this process of cutting what were known as the underwoods were then tied into faggots and left in the open air for a few months to dry out. They were then shipped off to the major towns and cities to be sold as firelighters.

Work in the woods, like many country tasks, tended to be seasonal in nature. Much of the cutting of underwoods, for example, took place during the winter months, and there was not always enough to keep on all those involved throughout the rest of the year. Seasonal employment has always been a factor in country life, particularly in the past when there have been no contractual arrangements of any sort between employer and employee. The result was that many men varied the work that they did enormously during the course of the year. Someone who spent the winter working in the underwoods might well find work in the spring and the harvest season on a local farm, and if he was lucky, for the whole of the rest of the year as well.

Certainly, many farms did have need of a considerable amount of casual labour at peak times of the year, and it was normal for a number of extra men to be taken on for a few weeks and put up in one of the outbuildings. A lot were Irish, who came over and travelled round finding work in different areas as it was required. But there were also local men who did all sorts of work throughout the year and thus scraped together a meagre living, with perhaps some help from the produce of an allotment or a small garden.

Often that part of the casual labour which was not local was either recruited by word of mouth, or perhaps at some form of show or agricultural fair. Towns like Stratford upon Avon held annual 'Mop Fairs' which were typical country fairs and also served as an unofficial labour exchange. The 'Mop Fair' was known widely as a place where farmers would come to find men for part of a particular season, and as a result it was the place where the migrant labourers of the Midlands came to line up work for the following weeks or months.

In the years after the War no farm workers ever really had proper holidays, except for the feast days at Christmas and Easter, and even those days were really like a normal Sunday when, whilst there was in theory none of the usual work to be done, time still had to be taken to feed all the livestock and make sure that all was in good order. Boxing Day was the one real holiday, when life on the farms, bar the essentials, stopped and everybody, rich or poor, went off to follow the hunt, or, as some farmers did, go shooting or fishing. Every other day of the year meant an early start and long hours.

Normally a cowman was at work the earliest, often rising at five o'clock and working through the day without much of a break. This usually meant that he worked a sixty-hour week or even more, for a wage which immediately after the War was normally only around two pounds per week. The ordinary farm labourer earned even less, perhaps only around 31 shillings per week. These were not the rates received by a young man; they were all that farmhands could expect to receive throughout their working lives. And, as has been seen, by the early twenties these wage levels were already falling.

There was, though, provision for overtime, which was often worked given the virtual round-the-clock nature of farm work. Normally extra hours were paid at 7 pence each for men, and at the various times of year, particularly during the harvest, when women were needed to help in the fields, they were paid 4 pence per hour.

The alterations to the National Insurance provisions after the First World War brought agricultural workers within their scope for the first time. The onus of arranging for payment to be made fell upon the farmer, who deducted the amount due from each of his employee's wages, and then had each man's book stamped by the appropriate authority.

Not surprisingly, with much of the farm work taking place out in the fields, most men ate lunch out there. In many places, they went to work with a rush basket on their shoulders with their midday meal in it. Standard fare was the top of a homemade cottage loaf — it was never sliced — with butter, a small piece of fat pork, or some cheese and perhaps an onion, washed down with a bottle of home-made beer. In some places men were more adventurous. If any building work was going on in the countryside, the workers would often gather mushrooms and cook them on a shovel over a small fire. And in the woodlands the men would often light a fire in cold weather and toast things or make hot drinks.

One of the most sought after jobs on the farm was doing the ploughing, regarded by many as rather an art. Ploughmen took tremendous pride in what they did, often holding competitions to see who could plough the straightest furrow. And it was indeed a very skilled task. A normal plough had one single cutting blade and was pulled by two horses. Not surprisingly, this combination was considerably less manoeuvrable than a modern tractor-pulled plough, and required a substantial turning circle at the end of each furrow. To solve this problem the normal practice was to plough what was known as a headland around the entire field, so as to make a kind of frame around the rest of the area to be ploughed. This enabled the horses and plough to be turned around after each furrow before continuing to plough.

Even doing this, though, did not make it particularly easy to plough a perfectly straight furrow. Those who could became renowned in a district, and young farmhands were eager to learn so that they could one day attempt the same.

Given the preponderance of the horse in farm work, every village or district had to have its blacksmith and forge, though few smiths were quite as colourful characters as the demon fast bowler of *England, Their England* might make us think. Even so, many were the mainstay of the local cricket team.

The local blacksmith tended to be a man of great resource, with skills well over and above those needed to shoe the local workhorses. Almost anything made from metal was within his capabilities, whether you needed a new wrought-iron gate or, believe it or not, a cigarette lighter — the speciality of one Sussex blacksmith. This service was vital to most farmers, who depended absolutely upon the local smithy for maintenance and repairs to what machinery they had. And of course there was the more specialised shoeing work, perhaps for the local hunters, hacks and racehorses. Almost invariably, the smith was a burly man with massive muscles. Some were the terrors of the men who ran the trials of strength at local shows, often able to bend large iron bars in their bare hands.

Many farm workers lived in tied cottages owned by the farmer, in conditions mentioned later. Whether they lived rent free depended very much upon the individual employer. Many paid nothing, but it was not unusual for a deduction to be made from the weekly wage to cover the cost of accommodation. Sometimes this close link between home and work could prove hazardous for the farm labourer. With few, if any, contractual guarantees of work, falling out with the farmer might well mean not only the sack but also being evicted from one's home. For those who suffered this fate, it was often difficult to avoid the fateful trip to the local workhouse.

It was not unusual for some of the workers on a farm to sleep in an outhouse and spend much of their spare time in the farm's kitchen or scullery. But the rest of the farmhouse was strictly out of bounds, and there were often no washing or latrine facilities provided for them. Sometimes there might be a copper provided in one of the other outhouses for their use, but even so it remained a fairly primitive existence. Of course there were exceptions, but they were generally rare.

Many farm labourers lived in tied cottages owned by the farmer, from which they could be evicted very suddenly. The cottages were usually tiny, perhaps with as few as two rooms, and often very primitive.

There tended to be little contact between the farmer and his family and the farmworkers who lived in the house and outbuildings except during the course of the day's work. Of course they were seen about the place, and often children would go out to talk to them, but otherwise it was a surprisingly separate existence given the proximity of living accommodation. The farmer's wife and children might well not even know the surname of the men who lived in their own backyard, referring to them always by their christian name.

In general the relatively well-off, middle-class farmer lived a comfortable existence, even though he also had to be out working during the long hours of farm activity. Most farmhouses were quite spacious by comparison with the farm workers' accommodation, and the majority enjoyed much better indoor facilities. If many still had a copper by the back door and an earth closet, even more now had their own bathroom and a fair degree of internal plumbing, although hot water still had to be heated up in the kitchen and poured into the bath.

Fewer houses and farms, though, had mains water, forcing them to depend upon pumped well water. And while many families enjoyed comparative luxury, some still used an earth closet right through the twenties and waited many years before they could enjoy the luxuries of modern plumbing.

Most farmers were sufficiently prosperous to have at least one living-in maid, though she tended to be the only member of staff for most families; the farmer's wife did much of the domestic work in addition to some tasks on the farm. It was not unusual, though, for there to be occasional staff as well, perhaps in the form of a local woman who came once a week to do the washing. Even so, in marked contrast to many more prosperous middle-class families in the towns, the woman of the house was constantly busy with practical work, and had less spare time to devote to charities and other popular middle-class pastimes for women.

Socially, the life of the farming family was somewhat of a contradiction. Generally speaking, their social status was that of a reasonably comfortable middle-class family, in so far as such things can accurately be assessed. But in the countryside life could be rather different to that of the middle-class family in the town, and this was certainly true of their social life. For instance, it was quite normal to find the middle classes and the lesser aristocracy mixing relatively freely. In the hunt they rode side by side, and attended together the parties that followed. The parson and his wife too could often be found dining at the table of the local lord of the manor. Of course, the great noble families tended to keep more closely to their own kind. But whilst in the cities and towns the classes tended to divide much more clearly and mix less freely, in the countryside there was often much more contact between the wealthy landowner and the working, middle-class farmer.

Which is not to say that the farming communities were snobbish. As is mentioned in the following chapter, there was far less actual social consciousness in the countryside than in the towns. And though there was clearly a gulf between farmers' families and the hands, who lived and ate in the same house in many cases, nevertheless the majority of farms were happy, if hard-working, communities. For instance, it was common for a farm to have its own cricket team, whether or not there were actually enough players to make up an eleven. Annual matches with neighbouring farms were eagerly awaited, and the excitement of the occasion was shared by everyone.

But improving lines of communications, largely through the arrival of the motor car and the telephone, the bus and the metalled road, were beginning to reduce the isolation of many country areas. A few country people were now city workers who caught the ever-faster train service into the urban areas each day. Many farmers now had sons and daughters who lived and worked in the cities and towns. The gulf between town and country was narrowing rapidly.

In the countryside itself things were changing. Already the horse was disappearing from the roads — it would not be long before the earliest tractor, cumbersome and expensive to begin with, would be improved into a machine which all farmers could afford. By the start of the 1930s that change was already gathering pace. And as the process of mechanisation got under way unemployment among agricultural workers, which had hitherto followed a seasonal and cyclical pattern, would become permanent and men would leave their birthplaces to seek out new opportunities in the towns. Their departure would mark the end of a way of life that had remained much the same for many generations, and the end of an era for the English countryside.

THE ENGLISH VILLAGE

Traditionally, a romantic aura suffuses one's image of the English village. One immediately pictures a pleasant village green surrounded by oak trees, with a group of white figures in the middle playing with bat and ball. In the postwar years, though, the idyllic world of *England, Their England*, insofar as it was apparent in real life too, was little more than a mask for a much harsher reality. As in the towns, the majority of country folk led what can best be described as a hard existence, based as much as possible on self-sufficiency.

The village served as the centre of a local community that might stretch for miles in all directions. Even so, it was a close-knit entity. Everyone knew everyone else, and there was little social snobbery, though as anywhere people tended to fraternise most with those who shared their background. The village was also the social centre for the district. It was there that everyone went to church on a Sunday, that the local sports teams played and that people gathered either in the pubs or at organised social events.

Furthermore, the village was vital as a service centre for the surrounding farmland. It was there that the blacksmith had his forge and the wheelwright worked. Most of all, there was the village store, which stocked all basic necessities and was an essential port of call for even the most self-sufficient of households.

The War itself had little effect upon life in the countryside and villages, except to take away some of the sons who might have one day tilled the lands for themselves. In the small villages the tragedy of the War was particularly deeply felt because of the close-knit nature of the community, even though many men stayed behind to keep the nation's food supplies going. Significantly, it was in the relatively poor country districts that the most money was raised to build memorials to those who would not return.

But otherwise little changed. The girls who had helped on the land during the war were gradually replaced by returning soldiers and by those of the next generation who went onto the land. Crops and machinery were much the same, as was the way of life which depended upon them. It was a way of life with much hardship and little reward, much as it had been for centuries, but few of the older country people would have willingly surrendered it to go elsewhere.

The ordinary agricultural worker had little recreation, apart from visits to the local pub. Very few had any money to spare after keeping their families going, and a fair amount of spare time was spent in the small gardens that surrounded the labourers' cottages on every farm, eking a few extras out of the ground to make the family resources go that bit further.

The majority of agricultural labourers lived in small cottages owned by the farmers, either provided free of charge or for a small rent. Often the cottages were tiny, with only

Villages were the focal points of country districts. It was there that everyone went to church on Sunday, that the local sports teams played, and that people gathered at the pubs or at organised social events.

one main room downstairs and a little kitchen attached, and one or two bedrooms upstairs. There would be no modern facilities at all: there would normally be an earth closet at the end of the garden, and all water was usually carried in from a well.

For most men their small garden was more than just a means to grow a little more food for the family. It was also an escape, and a way to gain a sense of achievement. Each year most villages held a flower show, and local people would work for many hours in their gardens to try to beat the next man in various competitions. In a sense it was a way for a man whose life was one of toil and survival to win a little success and a feeling of superiority.

As country people there was usually no problem getting hold of fuel for the fire inside because wood could usually be gathered from around about. Even so, many cottages were damp and draughty, if usually fairly soundly built, and the winters tended to be long and cold.

There was, of course, no electricity or mains gas in country areas, and lighting within houses was sparse, normally provided by oil lamps or even candles. There was no street lighting either, so that anyone going out at night would normally carry a hurricane lamp to find their way through the darkness, or sometimes a candle in a jam jar.

Many farm labourers' wives did all their cooking in a single big pot over the main fireplace in the cottage living room, although there was a small brick oven at the side of the fireplace for baking bread and cooking the occasional special dish. Normally, though, the family resources only allowed enough for a main meal which was a stew from the pot, and they ate bread and cheese or jam at other times of the day. Because of the nature of the work it was normal to eat the main meal in the evening, unlike urban working families who ate theirs in the middle of the day whenever possible.

In the summer months many families sought to ease the cramped state of their homes by moving part of it outside, the most common change being the transfer of the cooking pot from the fireplace in the living room out onto a brick grate outside the back door.

In spite of the cramped living accommodation, most families tended to be very close-knit. It was not uncommon for the whole family, whether adult or child, not to go out to the pub or to play during the evening, and instead stay by the fireside playing ludo or draughts. And, of course, low wages often dictated that men spent most evenings at home, saving up for the one weekly spree on a Saturday. Furthermore, most men had to rise at dawn the next morning to begin work, and in many cases the whole family would be in bed asleep by eight or nine o'clock at night. Even so, there was generally little animosity between parents and children, and families genuinely enjoyed spending the hours before bedtime playing games and chatting.

In most rural households, like in the towns, the father was very much the boss, and his word was effectively law. In fact, strong discipline in the home was a virtual necessity. Country families tended to be quite large — one Suffolk girl who left the countryside to go into service was the youngest of twenty-two children. But even in more normal cases, where there might be four or five children, conditions were so cramped that obedience was very important if the family were to maintain any sort of sanity at home.

A significant proportion of the rural population lived on smallholdings of a few acres, found dotted around most villages in agricultural areas. Perhaps combined with a part time or even full time job outside, and supported by a hard-working wife, a smallholder could eke quite a reasonable living by country standards out of his little piece of land. Many were, in fact, self-sufficient. Almost anything that could be made was made. In fruit-growing areas a small orchard of apple trees could provide enough juice to make a few barrels of cider to sell locally or to keep for consumption during the winter months. A beehive could produce enough honey and sugar, as well as beeswax, to meet the family's needs. Most people kept a pig or a few cattle, as well as hens to provide a regular supply of eggs. And the year's supply of vegetables would come from their smallholding.

Smallholders produced much of their own food as well. Each week there would be a baking day, and when the family pig was slaughtered for meat it would be smoked in a little oven at the side of the cottage and then cured for winter. Men brewed their own beer and made wine from anything that could be gleaned from garden or hedgerow.

Some things, of course, had to be bought in from outside — men would take their carts to the local railway station and buy chests of tea and sacks of sugar from dealers there. Salt, too, came by train in huge blocks, which were often then given to one of the children to break up into a usable form.

The majority of smallholders had no land for grazing livestock, given that most of what they had was needed for growing vegetables and keeping poultry and pigs. Generally, because there was so little traffic around, they solved this problem by simply turning cattle out onto the roads to eat on the verges and where grass had grown up between the gravel on the roads themselves. Most country roads were still unmade, and those cars that were already to be found in country districts made very slow progress.

There was never any problem in finding the cattle, even though they were seldom supervised. Generally led by one or two beasts, they tended always to follow the same routes and eat in the same places, making it easy for their owners to find them at the end of each day. Normally this was a job for a child after school.

All too often, it was the children who were the worst sufferers of the intensity of country life. Many got up early each morning to work before school, were then faced with possibly a long walk to the school itself, and then rushed home to continue farm work in their lunch breaks. Hardly surprisingly, they were often too tired to make much effort in classes during the afternoon, and teachers who realised the position they were in were generally reluctant to make them work harder in those lessons.

The problem was accentuated by the fact that many country people simply could not see the point of an education. Not really aware of the fact that there were opportunities outside the rural community for those who did well at school, they were reluctant to encourage their children's academic progress. To them, the education that was really necessary for the children was what was provided on the farm or in the home. Indeed, many put pressure on their sons and daughters to leave school as early as possible to begin what they considered their 'real' schooling. The brightest and hardest-working thus left first, since they were the ones that parents were keenest to have working at home.

The end result of all this was that country children at the end of the First World War tended to be less literate and less well educated than most of their counterparts brought up in the towns and cities. But this fact caught the attention of the education lobby and of the Department of Education and in the early twenties moves were made to make it more difficult for children to leave school too early by making it compulsory for them to have obtained an educational proficiency certificate beforehand. Though it did not solve the problem of the long hours, it did go some way towards improving standards among country children.

When children were not at school or helping their parents, they were usually to be found in the village or the woods playing games with friends. Children from farms well outside the villages tended to live a relatively isolated existence while they were still fairly young, and not until they grew older did they begin to go into the village on a regular basis and make friends of school acquaintances who lived there.

One of the great novelties of the twenties in farming areas was the arrival on the market of motorbikes that were within the price range of young men who saved any spare pennies out of their wages. A very small two-stroke bike, capable of doing ten or twenty miles an hour, could be bought for just under ten pounds, and for someone who worked hard and lived at home it was not an impossible dream. As more and more young men in a district got their own motorbikes, they took to travelling around on Sundays seeing the surrounding area. The bikes were never really powerful enough either for racing or scrambling in the woods — in reality they were little more than motorised bicycles.

Visits to the pub, though much looked forward to by the young farm workers, had to wait until they came of age at eighteen, even though there were few policemen around to check up. The landlords of the local pubs knew most people in the district, and were not to be fooled by young men pretending to be older than they really were.

Despite the widespread efforts towards self-sufficiency on the smallholdings around most villages in the better agricultural areas there was still need for a village shop or shops to cater for those who had no land, whether they be labourer, blacksmith or vicar. A typical village store sold virtually anything. At one end there might be a meat counter where you could order a slice off a large joint of meat, and to get there you might walk past shelves of ironmongery, racks of clothes and shoes, or anything else that the village might need. Normally there would also be a village post office which often had a telegraph facility.

Quite probably one of the village shopkeepers would have a large baking oven to produce bread for those householders who did not produce their own and in at least one village he always helped out the families who had a large joint of meat — perhaps for Christmas dinner — by cooking it for them if they had not room to do it themselves. Such was the nature of the close-knit community.

The result of this was that local people, with little disposable income, had very little need actually to go out of the village at all. Whatever service one was likely to need, it could be provided by someone within the community, and everything you were likely to want could either be cultivated at home or bought at one of the local shops.

A considerable amount of local produce was bought direct from the farmers themselves by the women of the village. This was particularly true where a family did not live right in the village and the wife did not want to spend too much time walking to and from the shops there. Except for those areas where someone local had already set up a milk round, milk was bought directly from the farmer. Eggs were bought virtually straight from the hen, and many other foodstuffs, such as mushrooms, could be easily gleaned from the country-side.

For the older generation, and often for the younger as well, the village community provided all the social life that country people either wanted or had time for. The majority of men spent their leisure time in the local pub, when they could afford it. A peaceful evening gossiping about local matters or playing darts with his mates was all that any older countryman really aspired to do when he was not working.

It was extremely rare, though, in contrast to the cities, for any of the local girls or women to be seen out at the pub. In the 1920s the country inn remained a male bastion, and it was not until considerably later that this began to change.

However, in the countryside the local inn was far more than just an entertainment centre or place for drinking. As often it contained the only large public room in a village

The majority of men spent their social life in the village inn. A peaceful evening gossiping about local matters, playing darts or, as here, bar skittles with his mates was all that any older countryman really aspired to when he was not working.

readily available for use, it became an important meeting point for all sorts of people. If a farmer or landowner needed a special job doing for which he had to amass a group of workmen for a day, he might put an advertisement in the local paper, or even in the pub window itself, to say that he wanted to meet anyone looking for a few days' work in the pub at a certain time. In that way he could gather together his work gang.

The pubs could also be important trading centres. They would tend to be open all day on market day so that farmers and millers could do business. Indeed it was often, much more than the market itself, the local corn exchange. Equally, if two people who lived a distance apart wished to do business over, perhaps, a herd of livestock, they might agree to meet half-way between their two homes, sealing the transaction in a pub yard somewhere on the way.

The pub was then, as indeed it often still is today, a place where property auctions took place, or equipment was bought and sold on an informal basis. At the centre of all this was the landlord. Normally a local man with a good knowledge of the surrounding country, he was the key to a lot of good deals. If somebody wanted to buy something, the landlord would usually know where it could be found. Equally, he might serve as an unofficial labour exchange, able to point the unemployed in the direction of a local farmer who was short-staffed or needed a gang of men for a one-off job.

By the twenties, though, the local inn had ceased to be a resting point for the traveller. In the past it had been the natural port of call on a long journey by coach or horseback. But by now the faster motor car had arrived, and with it the old trade, already reduced by the railways, dwindled away almost completely. The old inn was now just a public house.

Few pubs still brewed beer on the premises. The last few years of the nineteenth century had seen furious efforts by brewers to buy up pubs to secure extra outlets for their beer. This rush to obtain as many tied houses as possible had not been restricted to urban areas, and the majority of rural inns were now tied houses as well. Deliveries came out on horse-drawn drays from breweries in the local towns, and, as the twenties progressed, on motor lorries as well.

But socialising was far from limited to an evening in the pub. Every village had its parish hall, perhaps provided by a local benefactor, and the community organised frequent whist drives, beetle drives and dances there.

And, of course, there was the inevitable cricket team, to be found in almost every village and regarded as much as an English institution as the village itself. Each weekend during the long summer months villagers all over the country would pile into huge charabancs, capable of carrying perhaps an entire team in one load, and drive off to do battle with a neighbouring community on the village green or perhaps a lovingly tended cricket field on the edge of the village. There the blacksmith, the farmers, their labourers, and perhaps even the parson and the local squire, would gather together. Social divides that were few and far between in the countryside anyway completely disappeared to be replaced by a shared desire to outdo an old adversary. And even if there was rivalry, it was usually good humoured, and soon forgotten as the two teams repaired to the local inn to sink a few jars.

Football, too, was popular and inter-village matches frequent during the winter months. But it was less of a unifier in village life, being, as it is, much more the preserve of the young and fit, whereas on the cricket field there was no early retirement.

A great social innovation of the twenties in many villages was the setting up of the young farmers' clubs. These often began as what were known as 'calf clubs' in which farmers' sons could compete with each other to test their skills in raising cattle. Each young

A meet of the Heythrop, Oxfordshire. Country pursuits remained traditional, and when the hunt met everyone downed tools to follow the hounds, whether as a hunt member on horseback or on foot.

farmer kept a calf for a year, at the end of which there was a show at which they were judged. From this beginning the clubs became more and more socially orientated and gradually evolved into the young farmers' clubs that exist all over the country today.

One sporting institution in particular was common to the entire rural community, though: the local hunt was a way of life for everyone in the country. Although dominated by the wealthy farmers and landowners resplendent in their hunting pink when the hunt met, it attracted followers from all walks of life, and was regarded as a great event by everyone. There was none of the abhorrence of hunting that is prevalent today, so deeply was it rooted in rural life and lore.

Indeed, as was the case on the great aristocratic estates which are dealt with in the next chapter, the hunt and other bloodsports were at the centre of much of the social life of a large part of the country community, particularly that of the better off. While everyone mixed from time to time and effectively knew everyone else, the wealthy farmers and their families did not spend their evenings drinking in the pub with the labourers or at whist drives organised for the villagers. For them social life revolved around sporting life. The hunt might well be the only middle-class institution in a particular locality, and naturally through it events like the annual ball would be organised. Shooting parties or fishing also provided a focal point for rural society, and an excuse to hold a dinner party afterwards.

Of course this did not make the hunt particularly exclusive. It was funded by the wealthy farmers, over whose land it went, and they and the local landowners made up its committee and officials. But when the hunt met everyone downed tools and followed the hounds, whether as a hunt member on horseback or on foot.

Hare coursing too tended to be very popular in many rural areas, mainly because of the opportunities it offered for gambling. The sport involved the pursuit of a hare by two grey-hounds, with the victor being the first to force the hare to veer away from its chosen escape route. Whenever there was a sizeable coursing meeting bookmakers would come from miles around to take bets on the event, and whilst it was again the gentry who were the main participants, the whole of a neighbourhood would usually turn out to watch.

Because of the close-knit nature of the village and rural community intermarriage between families was inevitable and occurred generation after generation. Of course there was considerable contact between different villages in a particular locality, and being born in one did not mean that you would never never move away. But generally speaking most people had a large number of relatives in both their own village and the surrounding ones, and surnames tended to be very common. When there was a funeral, even if the deceased was not particularly well-known, crowds of people might turn out to attend the service, simply because he or she would have had so many relatives within easy walking distance of the church.

This widespread interrelationship is one definite reason for the fact that class differences were much less pronounced within rural communities than elsewhere. Of course there were still the gentrified farmers and their families who had little to do with the ordinary country folk, but otherwise there was little social self-consciousness in most villages. Wealth did not tend to divide individual members of the community from one another.

Naturally, different people had their own circles of close friends — for one thing, as we have seen, farm labourers in the pub would not immediately fraternise with smallholders — but the separate groups respected, tolerated and even occasionally socialised with each other. And above all they were all part of village life. There was little or none of the snobbery sometimes to be found in the cities. But some changes were afoot in the postwar years that would gradually break down the insularity of many villages. The most obvious of these came with the gradual introduction throughout the English countryside of bus services. At first these were sparse. In the immediate postwar years one Cheshire village had a single horsedrawn bus into Chester each day, and this was really no more than a large farm wagon with seats put in the back of it. But, as the twenties progressed, so motor buses became more and more common, at first on the more important routes between country towns, but then increasingly in more remote areas as well.

The possibilities provided by the growing bus services were unprecedented. Previously, a day trip of perhaps twenty miles to the nearest large town had been out of the question for most people. Now it could be done. The novelty was enormous for communities which had lived in semi-isolation. A day trip to town came to be regarded by many as almost a holiday, something to be looked forward to for days in advance. There were large markets that stayed open all day and well into the evening, shops with goods never before seen, and general merrymaking, particularly on market day which was when most people went to town. Normally this was on a Saturday.

In addition, increasing access to the outside world introduced new opportunities for entertainment. Perhaps the large town would have a cinema, or even a theatre. As the bus service improved, so these things became real possibilities. People who had never seen a motion picture now found that they could go into town for the evening and still get back in time for a good night's sleep before work the next day.

As the twenties passed, more and more people began to get cars for the first time, or to buy motor vans to replace the carts which they had always previously used for working. They too found their horizons broadened. In one Sussex village the local garage owner set up a small taxi service with a couple of charabancs for hire as well, and for the first time the cricket team could play matches well outside the locality.

In many senses such changes spelt the end of the village community as it had always been. The villages had always thrived as harmonious communities precisely because they were so insular. Indeed because of the interrelation of so many of the local people, they really were one large happy family, despite the relative hardship of country life.

But as that insularity was gradually broken down by change, so the perceptions of village people began to change as well. Now not all the young people left school at the age of twelve to go onto their parents' farm or smallholding. Some began to stay on into their teens, and a few even went to university.

For those who had to suffer the vagaries of the country economy, there was also a clearer idea of what could lie beyond in the towns and cities. There, job security did not depend just on the weather, so there was further migration out of the village communities. Then there was the beginning of a move by the more prosperous out of the suburbs into houses in the country where living conditions and environment were altogether more agreeable. Ever-increasing speed on the railways meant that commuting from well out in the countryside was no longer an impossibility, and indeed it began to get more and more common.

These trends were very slow, however, and perhaps scarcely noticed by those who lived in the villages in the twenties and thirties, depending upon the location of the particular village. But as the metalled roads arrived, together with the regular bus services that provided the link with the towns, so the nature of the villages began to change totally. Ultimately they would become an often ungainly amalgam of the retired, the local and commuting professional, and the remnants of the agricultural community that were not destroyed by the rapid mechanisation of the farms.

Yet in the years after 1918 most were still much as they had been for generations, close-knit communities with little social rivalry and a strong shared identity. The most drastic effects of change lay in the future, and for many a weekday journey to the neighbouring market town or on a Saturday night to a party some miles away was the furthest they ever went. Only horses and carts, with perhaps the occasional charabanc or car, would ever be seen going past the village green, and the lanes were so rarely used by motor traffic that they were perfectly safe for the cattle to graze in.

These were the last years before mechanisation set in, the final years of the hay wain and the prosperous blacksmith's forge. Indeed, for the traditional English village of folklore it was an Indian summer. And the death of the community as it had always been would lie not in the carved stone war memorial recently erected on the village green, but in the gradually encroaching menace of the tarmac.

Though much of England's countryside remained unaltered until as late as the 1920s, and some villages still only had grassy lanes to link them to the outside world, equally there were main roads, main lines and towns long established. Rural England and the slums and terraces of the cities were worlds apart, but on occasions they did meet, in industrial villages in the Midlands and North where agriculture and perhaps a coal mine existed alongside each other, or in the market towns which depended both upon their own businesses and industry, and the income brought from regular markets and the resale of produce to keep their economies going. They could be ungainly, yet relatively harmonious, communities in which rich and poor lived within a few hundred yards of each other, without the geographical divides created by the size of a city. Their reputation was often one of dullness and provinciality. In reality they were anything but that.

Most of England's small country towns had grown up as service centres providing for

The towns were the market centres for farming areas, where the farmers brought produce and stock for sale, and in turn bought those things they could not provide for themselves. Norwich Market in 1935.

agriculture what the limited resources of the village and the farm could not. The black-smith might be able to repair the plough, or perhaps even build a new one, but the more complex equipment came from urban workshops. The towns were also the vital market centres for farming areas, where the farmers brought produce and stock for sale and in turn bought those things they could not provide for themselves.

Not surprisingly, market day, whether weekly or monthly, was one of organised chaos in every town. This was particularly true of areas where agriculture was geared to stock raising rather than crop growing. In those cases the roads would become one great river of animals coming in to be congregated in thousands awaiting the auctions and the sales. If they were sheep matters became even worse as sheepdogs frantically tried to rescue their charges from becoming lost in the melee.

The streets would also be full of smallholders bringing their surplus to sell, of pedlars and quacks, and of those who had come to buy or simply to observe. Market day was usually on a Saturday, so those who worked in the small manufacturing businesses and finished work on that day at lunchtime would be in town for the market or drinking in the packed pubs. And of course all the local characters would be out on the streets, the drunks and the idiots, the jokers and the insane. With frequent dancing and partying in the town and the pubs at the end of the day, it was the time of the week when the whole community came alive. And in many towns one or two unlikely traditions still survived, to be seen amidst the market crowds, such as the town crier. Though not always resplendent in their uniform, they appeared, plus the obligatory bell, three or four times a week, perhaps to announce coming events to passers by or to proclaim some important message from the town council.

One of the features of the country towns which could create the atmosphere of market day, over and above just buying and selling between farmers, was their geographical compactness. In the cities the rich and the poor lived worlds apart. The families who occupied the slum streets had no contact with the prosperous areas where their betters lived, except perhaps through institutions such as the Sunday schools. But in a small town of perhaps fifteen or twenty thousand inhabitants the rich and the poor could not escape each other — often they lived virtually next door. In John Moore's *Elmbury*, his semi-fictitious account of his childhood in Tewkesbury, the author is born to a respectable middle-class family and brought up in a nice, reasonably-sized house. But right opposite is what he calls Double Alley, the filthiest street in the town. Here are the homes of all the least desirable members of the community. But there is no friction between the two, even though they are opposite extremes. Every town had its undesirable characters, and its poor streets, and respectable people might be reluctant to tread those streets at night. But even so the two worlds managed to exist side by side, without any strong degree of hostility or jealousy.

Which is not to say that the country town was not socially self-conscious. Indeed snobbery was as rife in these smaller communities than it was in any city. Indeed the very fact that the community in a small town was limited in numbers gave everyone a much better opportunity to compare notes on status both in work and financial standing, and made it more likely that people would be socially conscious.

Nowhere was this more evident than among those who had made good, who had risen from humble origins to perhaps running a small business or to a career in the professions. Once they had moved away from one of the humbler streets, contact with those origins would be slight, except perhaps insofar as most people would remain in occasional contact with relatives who had not made good. It tends to be true that the most socially conscious of all classes are those who have made their way up the social ladder and achieved a previously only dreamed of status. Nowhere was this more true than in the relatively constricted environment of the smaller country town. There people were especially conscious of who they had become and who they mixed with now.

It therefore became very important where one lived and what one did, even if poverty could be found living right alongside respectability. Some streets were regarded generally as being occupied by people who were of the lower orders. By contrast there were parts of the town which would be regarded as very much up-market. The key difference between this and the class divisions of the city was the narrowness of the divide. It was not a matter, as in the case of the majority of people who lived in the vast slum areas of the cities, of not knowing the land outside their neighbourhood. Instead rich and poor knew each other well, and the distinction between different streets and areas was all too clear.

Social consciousness was most evident among the women, perhaps because they had more time to contemplate status, and because of the rampant nature of gossip in the smaller communities of the country. In a town of 20,000 inhabitants there were sufficiently small numbers of people around for individuals not to be faceless, and for social advancement to be noticed and discussed enviously by the gossips. The women became very conscious of their social standing, shunning those who were not acceptable and trying to get into the circles of those who were more than just acceptable.

Men were less concerned about social status. Most could not escape their roots insofar as they continued to meet the lower classes through their work, whether they now had their own businesses, or had simply risen from the ranks to a managerial position. In most towns businesses were not large, and in a small firm it was likely that the boss would, from time to time, end up in the pub with his men, or would occasionally spend a day working with them or on a journey with them, all depending on the actual nature of the job being done. The women did not mix in the same way, and it was they who set the social rules of the community.

Those who had not 'up and come' but had been born into the wealthy classes were more subtle in their social attitudes, and it would certainly be wrong to suggest that the majority of the middle classes in the country towns of England were blatant social climbers. But there is no doubt that the nature of the communities, the fact that they were relatively insular given the fact that this was still prior to the modern era of mass communication — even though its foundations had already been laid — led to a very definite streak of snobbery.

This insularity was, of course, not nearly as extreme as it was in the multitudes of villages which lay away from the major transport routes. But even so, until the motor car became, during the 1920s, more than just the plaything of the rich, the towns remained primarily rural centres, unless they had a long-standing industrial base of their own, and so served two purposes. A typical example of this was the town of Long Eaton, near Nottingham. It had around eighteen thousand inhabitants, and was first and foremost a lace-producing town, producing goods for the textile markets in Nottingham. But it also served as a centre for the surrounding countryside, with businesses that catered for the needs of agriculture as well as the lace businesses. It had a weekly agricultural market attended by farmers from the surrounding area, and even one or two farms on its fringes. The growth of the local bus services after the War increased the prosperity of many such towns, and brought in new businesses and shops, as well as leisure amenities for the increasingly mobile country population. And as roads improved and motoring became more and more popular, so city dwellers began to take long trips out into the country at weekends.

The growth in road traffic along the main routes, and the increasing numbers of trippers who fled the cities at weekends in search of country air, spelt the end of many of the old village and town inns. In their place came the larger and more modern roadhouses, catering for the traveller, and often serving food of a quality that would draw in customers with cars from miles around. For years the anti-drink lobby and many licensing justices had been working to reduce the often enormous numbers of pubs per head of population, and the popularity of the new roadhouse merely served to encourage the decline of the smaller country pub in more developed rural areas. Brewers were only too keen to offer to surrender the licences of two or three of their older pubs, which probably made relatively small amounts of money, in order to secure a licence for a new roadhouse. It is ironic that in later years the cars and charabancs which were to bring custom to the new roadhouses began to seek out the more off the beaten track villages which did not give up their old pubs. It didn't take the drivers and passengers long to realise that they preferred the character of the old inn to the huge bars of the roadhouse.

And as the process of mechanisation spread through the countryside, and new industry appeared to service it, so the country towns themselves lost much of their rural character. A market where the farmers drove in motor wagons full of livestock had less atmosphere than one where for hours in advance the lanes and roads around were full of cattle in droves on their way to town. The city became closer as transport continued to improve, and many towns within striking distance of major population centres began to develop a commuter population. Gradually, the character of the towns began to alter. For them the modern era was dawning.

ON THE GREAT ESTATES

Throughout her history England has always been a land of great estates, dominated by a few hundred families who wielded much of the nation's political and economic power, and from which almost all politicians, senior army officers and other men of state have come. The age-old concept of primogeniture, which ensured that the eldest son inherited all, was the key reason for the continuing dominance of the landed aristocracy. In other countries, where tradition dictated that each son should receive an equal share of the father's property, most of the great landed estates had been broken up long before the start of the nineteenth century.

In 1914, though extension of the franchise and the growing wealth of the middle classes had deprived the great families of England of much of their political weight and had relegated the House of Lords to a second-class debating chamber, the supremacy of the aristocracy in much of the countryside remained relatively unscathed. But the next decade was to mark a major turning point for the aristocracy and their estates. The worst blow was the War itself. Among the flower of youth which died in Flanders were the eldest, and indeed many of the younger, sons of some of the great families. By 1918 there was often no longer an heir to inherit the estates.

Equally severe was the effect of economic and political change. Since 1894 there had been some degree of liability upon the estates of the dead. Estate Duty, as it was known, was chargeable upon all property, whether land, money or valuables even if, in the case of land, it had been settled upon a close relative for the duration of his or her life. In the years immediately after its inception the level of duty payable was relatively low, but by 1914 the cost of the social policies of the Liberal government had been met by tax increases, including a hefty rise in Estate Duty. Before 1908, on an estate of a million pounds, the amount payable was 8 per cent. In 1914 that had almost doubled, and by 1918 the cost of the War had pushed the rate up to 30 per cent. To the landed aristocracy the growth in this duty was a major blow, not so much because the large amounts payable upon the death of the head of the family were unaffordable, but because of the nature of their wealth. Much of this was tied up in capital assets, particularly land. So, whilst the money was there, it might yet prove almost impossible for a family to find enough cash to pay a debt to the Inland Revenue, which for a large estate might well amount to several million pounds. Often there was little alternative but to sell assets to raise the money, and frequently this meant that all or part of the estate had to go.

95

Many country houses had been built for the nobility or the new plutocracy in better times, when wages and running costs had been lower. By the 1930s, a good number were beginning to feel the effects of soaring costs.

Economic conditions were also changing. The War had dramatically increased both prices and wage levels. It had been a time of boom for industrialists, but for the landed and their private means life was less easy. In the years after the War land was paying a return substantially below the base rate offered by banks, and so in real terms the aristocractic landowner was actually losing out. As a result there was an increased tendency to sell up one or more of the family estates and to convert the proceeds into bonds and equities able to provide better income.

And of course there was the problem of the country establishments themselves. All had been built for the nobility in better times when wages and running costs were lower. One simply couldn't afford any longer to maintain a staff of twenty or more in both town and country, as well as the vast number of outdoor servants needed to keep a country estate in good order. Not that it was any longer certain that a suitable staff could be found. Young people were, as will be seen, less inclined than previously to go into service, and without spending money to improve the servants' quarters one could not hope to attract a better kind of employee.

In short, for many families there was every reason to sell off all or part of their estates, and many did. More land changed hands in the postwar years than at any time since the Norman Conquest, as all over the country old families sold up. In many cases they didn't sell their entire estates, preferring instead to raise money by selling farms to the sitting tenants or to other local people. Most estates were divided into farms, which made it possible to sell off parts without totally destroying the whole. Many families did sell their country houses as well though, often to the *nouveaux riches* who, having made fortunes from their War effort, were keen to acquire social respectability by buying such status symbols.

Where the old estates remained untouched there were still some internal changes. As the years went by progressively fewer people were employed both in the house and on the estate. Even the wealthiest landowners made cutbacks. There were fewer men in the gardens, in the woods, and fewer gamekeepers, although by today's standards the work-forces in these jobs were still substantial.

In those days the country estate was managed from an estate office by a local agent who acted as the owner's permanent right-hand man in all affairs in the district. Often the agent was from an aristocractic family himself. A typical occupant of the position might be younger son who had joined the army for some years and then taken up the agent's job in retirement. Once on an estate his role would be much the same as that of a managing director in business, overseeing and co-ordinating the work of a number of independent departments, as well as representing the aristocratic owner, who would frequently be visiting elsewhere or be at his town house. Normally the agent would live on the estate, often in a smaller house belonging to the family but not used by them. He would have his own household provided by the estate, as well as a chauffeur to drive him around. Generally the agent was a well-liked and respected man — few were tyrants and most treated their staff well. There were a few, though, who were less amiable, and often acted as overlords in their own right, with little compunction about the way they treated local people. But they were small in number, relics of a bygone age. By the twenties, with many being ex-army officers, the experience of war had broken down many old barriers and fostered a new spirit of broadmindedness. At the turn of the century there were agents who would enter houses as and when they pleased and horsewhip local people. In the twenties such things belonged to the past.

Outside the estate office there is no doubt that, as they had really always done, it was the gamekeepers who dominated the estate hierarchy. Most landowners used their estates primarily for hunting and shooting, and the social trappings that went with them. The keeper was therefore the lynchpin of the owner's interest in his estate. As a result the keeper's word was law. If someone was doing something that was going to affect the game, the keeper could have them moved elsewhere. If, for example, the farm hands were working on some land over which they were going to shoot the next day, one word from the keeper sufficed to clear the place at once. His authority was recognised throughout the estate and, as a result, by ordinary folk, the keepers were regarded as rather aloof, with almost a kind of mystique around them. It was a mystique altogether more refined than in the era, perhaps a century earlier, when the keeper could be a tyrant, ruthless to local people, and wholly above the law since, through his master, he effectively *was* the law. By the 1920s this no longer held true, but the keeper's authority still left him an individual to be feared and respected. Indeed, he often commanded much more respect than the local village policeman.

Most large estates still employed a large force of keepers, perhaps as many as twenty to keep the game well stocked, policed and ready to be shot. But the policing role was one considerably lessened by the passage of time. Higher living standards in the towns in particular had ensured that fierce battles between gangs of poachers and an army of defending keepers were really a thing of the past. For the average estate gamekeeper, life was more oriented around breeding game to keep the estate well stocked than anything else.

Breeding in those days was a highly labour-intensive occupation, which accounted for the great number of keepers employed on each estate. Chicks were bred in coops set out in a suitable field. They and their mothers had to be fed some four times daily, and moved round a couple of times as well. This had to be done in all weathers and, with few men yet enjoying the luxury of wellington boots, even on a warm summer's day heavy dew in the long grass ensured that each man got wet through every day on the job. Furthermore, many hours were spent in mixing large quantities of feed for the brooding hens. Without modern, specially prepared feeds, this task was of enormous importance since the successful raising of as much game as possible was regarded as a great art and one which was individual to each keeper. Every man had his own idea about how best to feed this year's mothers.

In fact, the process of rearing new birds often stretched the resources of a team of keepers so much that extra help had to be brought in from other parts of the estate. Because of the problem posed by foxes and other vermin, there had to be somebody on guard around the clock. Often even a large force of keepers had difficulty doing this, as well as keeping up with all their other duties, and could only manage with assistance from other estate workers.

Vermin control was another important part of the keeper's work. In most places rabbits were the commonest pest, dealt with either by setting traps or by sending ferrets down into the warrens. Many foxes were dealt with by the local hunt, but they too were still a problem.

By the 1920s the majority of estates had allowed their deer herds to diminish by not restocking them. This was generally a deliberate policy, since it was becoming increasingly difficult to keep an estate properly enclosed. The chief culprit was the motor car. The affluent aristocracy now wanted to be able to drive up and down the long drives of the country's stately homes without the hindrance of deer gates by the lodge. And without those gates there could be no deer. In any case, deer were more a decadent luxury than game in the real sense. It was all very pretty having hundreds of the elegant beasts grazing in the park, but shooting them really wasn't on. It was a challenge to shoot magnificent stags on hillsides in Scotland, but in one's own front garden, so to speak, where they were too tame to run away, hardly so. Instead, most landowners shot pheasants and other game birds, according to the season.

Shooting parties for the gentry were more than sporting occasions — they were aristocratic, or would-be aristocratic, social gatherings as well. The men's shooting clothes had changed hardly at all since before the Great War, but a marked change had overtaken the women's.

Shooting was probably the prime country pastime of the English nobleman in the 1920s, although by no means all of them participated. During the seasons of the various kinds of game there would be shooting weekends all over landed England. Some men might only shoot at home, but many more spent a weekend on each of their friends' estates each year. In that sense it was more than a sport, as much a social exercise in fact, a reason for an aristocratic gathering.

When the shooting party went out it was accompanied by a team of keepers and beaters who put up the game, that is, made the birds fly so that the sportsmen could have a shot. It would be the keeper's responsibility to ensure that any birds shot were gathered up and brought back. After a quick glance at the result of a successful shoot, the guests would be off in search of more, and then the next time the day's results would be seen would be when they were served up at table, perhaps the same evening.

The shooting party was an impressive sight. Each of the aristocratic sportsmen would have his own attendants to load the guns, and to carry cartridges. All the keepers and beaters wore their own particular livery — on the Grosvenor estates near Chester, one of the old keepers remembered wearing green velvet, white breeches and a gold-braided hat, and the beaters were dressed in white smocks and red felt hats. Suddenly appearing out of a wood, they had an almost feudal appearance.

Relations between the keepers and their masters were generally courteous, though most of that generation of nobility, while no means patronising and tyrannical, tended to be rather aloof in the presence of estate staff. They were briefly polite rather than ready to have a brief chat. This was less true of the younger generation. It was the keeper's job to teach the young gentlemen of the house how to handle a gun and about the habits of game. Here, inevitably, relations were much more friendly.

It was the keeper's job to teach the young gentlemen of the house how to handle a gun and about the habits of game. For ordinary country folk, shooting was mainly restricted to rabbits, vermin, ferreting, and a certain amount of poaching.

On most estates there was a home farm, run by a manager directly responsible to the estate office, and employing perhaps thirty to forty men.

But, the keepers and the staff in the house apart, estate workers seldom saw much of their aristocratic employers. The keepers only had a higher profile than the rest because of the important part they played in the upkeep of the estate and the maintenance of income from it, and also in the actual social life of the nobility. Almost alone on the estate, they were direct personal servants as well as workers. Although other workers were often well known to their employers, contact was usually infrequent.

Although one of the less visible jobs on the estate, the largest group of employees was almost universally to be found working in the woods. In order to keep hundreds of acres of prime woodland in good condition, and also to carry on a fair trade in timber, mostly to provide for the needs of the estate, there were often up to 100 woodsmen employed at any one time. Teams of men were also needed to tend the vast gardens and kitchen gardens to be found on every estate. Almost all the house's vegetables were provided by the kitchen gardens. Of course, the main gardens had, for social as well as aesthetic reasons, to be immaculate, and it was not unusual for there to be fifty gardeners working in the greenhouses and outside.

Elsewhere there would be woodsmen and craftsmen attached to the clerk of work's department, whose job was to ensure that buildings, fences, gates and such were kept in good order. If the aristocratic owner was a racing enthusiast, the estate might have its own stud farm, and perhaps a private racecourse for training, all of which of course needed staff.

On most estates there was a home farm, run by a manager directly responsible to the estate office, itself often employing thirty or forty men. And naturally there was the staff in the house itself, attending to all the needs of the family. Here there were chefs, maids of various kinds, valets, footmen, butlers, chauffeurs, grooms to look after the family's own horses, night-watchmen and so on. In all there might be two or three hundred people in a district employed by the local estate, as well as numerous others who depended directly upon the estate for their livelihood. At night the lanes were as full of men returning home to their neighbouring villages as the streets of a factory town might be at the end of a working day. Simply, the estate dominated the entire area.

Indeed it was very probable that the landowner actually owned all the surrounding villages. Where most small farms had a handful of tied cottages, he might have hundreds. Most of these were in the villages, though there were a few, more isolated cottages dotted around the estate, many of which were occupied by keepers.

Interestingly enough, the social divisions of the city were partly reflected in the great estates and the handful of villages dotted around them. One village might well be the one where the foremen and the senior staff lived, another the preserve of the labourers. Not that this divide was in any way as pronounced as it might be in the towns, since on the estate everyone knew everyone else. But even in the much more egalitarian countryside it did exist.

All in all the local landowner dominated the district with a kind of overlordship which maintained a strong air of feudalism, over and above mere ownership. As he had done throughout almost a millenium, the lord provided the living of the local churches and their parsons. He was the chief benefactor of the district, providing charity and welfare where it was needed. The estate often ran sick clubs or clothes clubs. Each worker would subscribe a few coppers each week to a fund controlled by the estate office, which was supplemented by a contribution from the estate itself. Then if one became ill, the cost of medical treatment was borne by the fund, and an allowance would be paid to keep wife and family going while the worker made good his recovery. Clothes clubs were intended to cater for the unfortunate reality that few country folk could afford new clothes. Once again, the coppers were collected and supplemented, and once or twice a year the fund would pay out a benefit to all its subscribers. Then, and only then, was there a sudden rush into town and the clothes shops.

And the feudal bond between lord and peasant, albeit rather more refined than in the past, remained largely intact as well. Hundreds of people, enjoying a not particularly high lifestyle, lived and worked amidst almost unbelievable wealth, splendour and decadence, without batting an eyelid. Contrary to the general, nationwide trend away from simple acceptance of the way things were, on the great estates things remained much the same. The aristocracy were genuinely respected, viewed almost with affection, and they merited it. Nobody really questioned their right to all they had. It was a little relic of feudalism which survived into the twentieth century.

Other feudal traditions had largely disappeared. In all but a few places the common land had been enclosed, leaving the majority of villagers with nowhere to graze their one or two animals. But this did not always prevent the keeping of livestock in the estate villages. Many nobles, conscious of the ways of life of the countryside, were happy to rent out one decent-sized field for a small amount to villagers for common grazing. Which led to what must have been one of the more amusing spectacles of the countryside. Each night, in many villages, one of the local women would go up to the shared field to bring the cows home. As the mixed herd meandered its way down through the village, one by one the cows would peel away from the rest. They all knew their own way home.

The influence of the aristocracy pervaded almost all parts of the lives of those who lived on or around the estates, and that influence depended very much upon the whim of the particular landowner. He could still control much of the country people's relatively limited social lives in so much as he dictated how often dances could be held in the village hall, or perhaps whether alcohol was to be allowed at social events. Obviously there was alcohol in the village, because of the inevitable pub, but a strict nobleman often ensured that dances and whist drives were teetotal affairs.

But the end of the First World War marked a watershed for the great estates, and not only because of changing circumstances for the aristocracy. The men who came home from the War were no longer willing to live the relatively mundane life that the old estates offered. Not all the aristocracy were able to adapt to this — one Cheshire man recalls his return from four years and seven months' fighting in France only to be told by his employer that he had not yet completed an apprenticeship and so would have to be paid a boy's wage rather than a man's. After the experiences of the trenches he was unwilling to accept this, and quit within a few weeks. Others could not take the country life after the excitement and comradeship of the army, and many went off to join the police force or take jobs in the towns.

Those who remained in the estate villages and their old jobs found a way of life little changed but beginning to change. As the years passed the influence of the landowner did begin to wane, although it was a very gradual process. And, as already mentioned, the trend was much less pronounced here than elsewhere — the nobility continued to enjoy enormous respect, although progressively less power.

While this change was very slow, relations between the estate workers altered more rapidly. Many old estate workers could look back to a time when, despite the fact that there might be a wealth divide in that the bosses might live in a different village, there was little or no snobbery or real concern about social status. Everyone worked on the estate for the lord, and in such conditions status became less relevant. Of course there were differentials in terms of work, but within the communities on the estate equality was a way of life. Then the War began to change this. Higher wage levels resulting from wartime inflation meant that estate workers had more money than ever before, although often ultimately to their cost since high wage levels were a prime cause of considerable staff redundancies in the postwar years as the aristocracy tried to reduce its overheads. Then, for the first time, people became conscious of material and social status. Having had a taste of increased wealth, albeit on a small scale, people wanted more. The mentality of keeping up with the Jones's appeared. In the eyes of the older generation of estate workers it ruined happy communities. People had always mucked in to help each other out. Now there was less of a spirit of co-operation. People became less willing to depend and be depended upon. And with that, a part of the old community spirit disappeared for good.

The First World War dealt a death blow to the England of great estates and landed aristocracy. Many estates were broken up, others acquired by people whose money came from commerce and industry, and who had no traditional ties with the countryside. Though many estates weathered the economic storms of the 1920s, and some of the old landed families survived with their ancestral heritage intact, the heyday of life on the estates was over. All saw their staff contract, and few escaped having to sell off some part of their vast acreage. There was still some life in landed England, but in reality its time had come. Those who returned from the War found the world in which they had grown up little changed on the surface, retaining much of its old character and traditions. But it was soon apparent that the old world had gone and a new one arrived.

The World of
the Wealthy

HIGH LIFE

It is, sadly, inevitable that throughout history the contribution of ordinary people to the society of their day is somewhat irrelevant. Almost invariably, it is the action of the few rather than of the majority that shape the perceptions of those who come after. It is all too easy to see the 1920s as the era of Evelyn Waugh's 'bright young things', living a life of gay abandon and loose morality, or to think of it solely in terms of the more intellectual yet equally 'free' life of the Bloomsbury set. In reality, though, each group was fewer in number and less influential by far than we perhaps imagine.

In fact the upper classes, whether 'upper' through birth or wealth, tried very hard after the end of the War to re-create the Indian summer of the Edwardian era. And away from the most prominent circles of the nation, thousands of middle-class imitators, social climbers extraordinaire, desperately strove, often in circumstances bordering on the ludicrous, to match the degree of respectability embodied in those who featured weekly in journals like the *Tatler*.

Those who tried to re-create the society of the prewar era found things much changed, though. Many of the old families were decimated by the War, perhaps losing all the younger male members at the front. Furthermore, as has already been seen, many of them were facing an economic crisis that would break up ancestral estates and leave many of the old landed families living a much humbler life than they would ever have dreamed of a century earlier.

In fact, this decline of influence was simply the continuation of a trend which went back through most of that previous century, although the War brought change about much more rapidly than would probably have been the case otherwise. At the beginning of the nineteenth century Britain was still dominated by the few hundred great landowner families who held both political and economic power and dominated high society and its institutions.

But gradually during that century the power structure of the country altered and, as a result, opened up previously exclusive social circles to a new generation of entrepreneurs who made money in business and then, perhaps, found a seat in Parliament, bought up a small country estate and sent their children to the best schools. Often it was the second generation of this new class who achieved a high degree of respectability in society — the father might remain something of a rough diamond despite his fortune. But the public school education introduced his children into a world unknown to him.

This is not to say that by the 1920s the landed aristocracy had lost all its power, influence and glamour, though in terms of politics and prosperity this was near to being true. In social terms a title and a solid background, preferably in a family which could be traced way back, was still highly desirable. It was still very much a pinnacle of social prowess to be seen hobnobbing with dukes and duchesses and attending glamorous balls at the great town houses of London during the 'Season' or going to house parties at large country houses.

The Season was the focal point of society life. Starting in February, it continued on into the early summer until such time as people began to leave London to go to events like Henley regatta, before heading off to the country or abroad for holidays. Effectively, it coincided with the time of year that the landed aristocracy and the upper classes had always spent in London; traditionally they arrived from their country homes after Christmas and remained in town until the holiday months. It was a time of endless parties and 'At Homes', a time for socialising amongst a group which still largely existed on unearned income and which was rarely in the same place at once. It was also the time, as will be seen, for introducing younger members of a family into upper-class social life, particularly the girls, who did not normally attend university and were not expected to enter life outside the family circle through jobs as the young men did.

But things weren't the same after the War, not just because of the young aristocrats who did not return, but because of the hard-faced men, as John Maynard Keynes branded them, the *nouveaux riches* who had made vast sums through their business interests during the War, and now had to be absorbed into the social elite. It was not a happy development for the older families, who saw values and standards sacred before the War begin to evaporate. To them the new rich simply did not know how to behave. They were regarded as upstarts by those who knew better, and many found their manner abrasive. There is a wonderful story of a leading London department store owner, newly entered into London society, meeting the immensely wealthy and popular Lord Rothschild at a drinks party, approaching him rather patronisingly, and demanding to know the price of money in the City. To this the financier gave a curt response before adding, 'And what's the price of piss pots in the Tottenham Court Road?' They were worlds apart. And for those who knew better, these new members of the upper classes were often considered beyond the pale. London society, for a time, became an uneasy amalgam.

This arose largely because such things as etiquette and speech were still regarded as a vital sign of breeding. The aristocracy, and indeed the aspiring middle classes which imitated them, have always tended to exclude those who did not conform to norms of behaviour. You had to be the right sort of person to receive the invitations that all sought desperately, and in the Edwardian era there was little trouble in this respect. The upwardly mobile had learned to behave at Eton or Harrow, and had little difficulty in fitting into their background as they grew older. But after 1918 values changed. There was no question but that money now talked as loudly as anything, particularly as the economic position of the aristocracy declined. Society became much more open, and those with money found themselves able to move in circles previously unknown. Before the War, for example, only the great families had enough money or had the huge London town house necessary to give parties. And if you didn't give parties, you wouldn't be invited to them. After the War, the families who had made their money in commerce and made the first step to respectability by buying a country house began to make the second. Increasingly, they began either to buy town houses or to take them for the season. Then the invitations could circulate, and they had arrived.

Later, the *Tatler* also suggested a reason for the transition of power in society from birth to riches. Charity had always been a cornerstone in upper-class activities, with amateur dramatics and charitable balls frequently being held in the great houses to raise money for the needy. In the years after the War such events were increasingly co-ordinated through a professional charity organiser, and it was only inevitable that they would go to where the money was for the organisation of some of the great annual events.

The increasingly open nature of society made it very much more competitive than it had been before. Gaining entry to such traditionally highly regarded enclaves as the Royal Enclosure at Ascot or being presented at Court became even more sought after.

Equally, everybody wanted to feature in the pages of either the *Sketch* or the *Tatler*. By such criteria was one's status in society judged. *Punch* published a very cutting article which summed up the situation perfectly: according to this to be at the bottom of the social ladder was to appear rather inconspicuously in a large photographed group of guests at some social event or other (at that time, none of the lesser guests were named in the caption — only those well known in society merited a mention). The next step up was when the young socialite was one of those named in such a picture as being 'among others present'. Promotion from here came when a caption described one as 'the well known', or 'the much sought-after', and relegated other guests. For most this was the summit of social achievement.

But for many it couldn't last. There were those young figures in society who went on to great things, either in public life, which kept them in the society spotlight, or by just becoming a rich and successful socialite who gave all the right parties. But many of those who passed through the pages of the glossy magazines soon went back to being yesterday's man or woman. Many married, and once the wedding pictures, and perhaps one of the first child, had appeared they were never heard of again. Beyond the altar the fascination of who was going to catch whom disappeared, and attention turned elsewhere.

Interestingly, although England was still very much a male-dominated country, despite the efforts and achievements of prominent ladies such as Lady Astor, society itself was very much dominated by women. The same was also true of upper class families and homes, in stark contrast to much of the country at large. Popular soirées or 'At Homes' were invariably given by hostesses, and it was they who organised both the grand balls and the house parties in the country later in the year. Very probably this originated in the very busy life led by their husbands, many of whom would have been involved in politics or in running businesses. He had his interests outside the household, and the rest of the family were scarcely involved or informed about them. But it was the wife who ran the household, whether it was disciplining children or servants, interviewing new staff, or arranging the family social life. The woman ran up the bills and the man paid them. She also tended to dominate in the lives of children, with the possible exception of arranging a son's private education. With many boys going to their father's old school, it was generally his responsibility to attend to this. But young girls were very carefully watched by their mothers as they grew older. It tended to be the mother who introduced possible friends, who arranged schooling and then eventually acted as chaperone when her daughter finally 'came out'.

After leaving school, and perhaps spending some time at a finishing school, the daughter would become a debutante. Essentially this meant that she made her first appearance outside the family circle and away from her relatively sheltered upbringing. The debs, as they were known for short, were paraded by their mothers at the social events of the Season, the great balls and the dinners, to meet possible suitors and to make friends and become a part of adult social life. Debs were almost celebrities for a season, given glamour

Everybody wanted to feature in the pages of the Sketch *or the* Tatler. *By such criteria was one's position in Society judged.*

treatment wherever they went. The next year they might just be one of the crowd. It is debatable whether the whole process was just a sophisicated marriage bureau, or whether it was a social exercise. But the reality was probably a mixture of the two. While many did find husbands quickly, many just made friends. Essentially, it was their passport into adult social life. Young men went into business or the professions to find their feet in life, but the girls didn't usually work and for them coming out was the only way to establish oneself as an adult in society.

Each deb was presented at court, even though the monarch was less evident in society as a whole. The presentation was a fairly mundane ritual, though, and scarcely more exciting than an investiture today, except of course for those involved. They had to queue in the Mall in advance, before being ushered into the Palace into a room almost like a cinema. Everybody took a seat, then one by one went up to the King, curtsied, shook hands, and retreated.

There were a number of professional hostesses who undertook to chaperone a young girl in society, and take her to all the leading parties during the Season. Even as traditional constraints on the lifestyles of the young were being relaxed throughout much of the country, attitudes within society remained very rigid. A young man could not take a girl out on his own: a chaperone had to be present always, at every moment. Those who managed to snatch a few minutes alone together were the fortunate ones.

Away from mainstream society life in London during the Season and at the grander balls, the chaperones were less evident. This was also true of house parties. Then parents mixed groups of young people who made their own entertainment, perhaps dancing to a gramophone or a small band, or playing billiards or snooker. So, while girls in particular were carefully watched by their parents, particularly as they grew older, so the watchful eye became less eager. It had to be acknowledged that, once adults, they could not always be treated like children. In general, though, the concerns of mothers about their daughters were not necessary. Though there was some degree of sexual activity within the single sex public school system, and there were inevitably those young men who went out to have a good time, mixing with women from outside their own circle in society, in general the young led a chaste existence.

Nonetheless the worst could, and occasionally did, happen. If ever a young lady happened to step out of line and have an affair with someone, and the worst possible scenario resulted and she became pregnant, the answer was a quick trip to Paris — under the conditions of the utmost secrecy. Of course, though, few things ever remained secret for long, and it was not long before rumours began circulating in society circles about a fallen girl. In reality, it was little different from the street gossip of the slums, where word soon passed round through the matriarchy. But the wealthy did at least have the discreet trip to Paris as a way out. It almost became a cliché. Paris was in fact chosen mainly because abortion was still illegal in Britain.

When it came to standards amongst the upper classes, the young man still had very much the best of it. If a girl got herself into trouble, her reputation was stained in the social circles in which she moved unless the fact could be kept very quiet. But a young man who perhaps got to know a few actresses and had a good time was merely regarded as sowing his wild oats. Perhaps he might not be quite right for one's daughter, but he was still a welcome guest at a weekend party.

Some of the aristocracy did in fact lead a wild life, particularly if they had the money to support such a lifestyle. On one occasion a young noble who spent a lot of time in a villa in the South of France was on his way down there and stopped off in Paris for a few nights. There he went to the theatre to see a play starring one of France's best-known and most beautiful actresses. After the play he invited her to dine with him, and then asked her to come on down to his villa with him. When she protested that she was under contract at the theatre and could not leave, he simply passed the matter on to his lawyers and they duly departed. Buying out the contract and wining and dining her for six weeks of passion on the Riveria was reputed to have cost him £60,000.

Yet even within the fairly rigid moral confines of society, where young girls were almost always chaperoned by their mothers or by another older woman, there was nonetheless a sharp decline in morality after the end of the War. There can be no doubting the influence of the War in this. Young couples, faced by the reality that leave was limited and that many went to the front and did not return, asked each other 'Why wait?' And many didn't. Furthermore, because of the War family ties were looser, since many girls were themselves actively involved in the War effort, perhaps in the various women's corps or as members of medical teams, so there was much greater contact between the young of both sexes away from the family eye. Old barriers crumbled because they simply weren't around at the time. And when War ended an entire generation of the young, or at least those who had survived, returned, as their working-class counterparts did in their communities, with a changed view of sexuality and morality.

Certainly this was a stark contrast to what had gone before. In the Edwardian home the young were always brought up to believe that one simply didn't do that kind of thing with one's friends or people in one's social circle. It was as taboo as incest, and in general nannies brought their protégés up to regard the whole thing as being rather 'rude'. After the War this did begin to change, though it should be emphasised that the change was not as dramatic as some historians have suggested, or as the surviving image of people like the Bloomsbury set would have us believe.

Homosexuality, though widely present in the public schools, was very much frowned upon in upper-class circles. Though homosexuals did reach high office and hold prominent places in society, they did so by remaining particularly discreet. If they failed to do so it could lead to ruin. Lord Beauchamp was exposed to the King as a homosexual in the early 1930s, and was forced to leave the country under threat of prosecution. (Homosexual intercourse was, at that time, a criminal offence.) The King, on discovering the truth about Lord Beauchamp, is said to have exclaimed, 'I thought men like that shot themselves.' Many people with homosexual tendencies managed to cloak them from the eyes of society as a whole through 'open' marriages, many of which were in themselves very sincere and strong. Perhaps the most famous of these was the marriage of the writer Harold Nicolson and Vita Sackville-West, which was outstandingly successful in spite of both of them having homosexual affairs.

For the young man in London society, entry into the right social circles was very much less organised than for the girls. The difference was that most went to university before seeking a career, perhaps in the City, in one of the professions or in a government post. Those who did not go to university would perhaps join the armed forces, or start work in the family business or set to managing the family land if any remained. So, essentially, it was their career which made the important break from home.

By contrast, young girls from wealthy backgrounds who didn't need to work were often not allowed to work, something which annoyed many of them, particularly those who had been active during the War. But this annoyance was very short-lived, since the majority of girls married relatively young, and thenceforward mostly spent their time either out in the country for long periods socialising, out riding or hunting, perhaps playing tennis or croquet with friends, or whiling the hours away with needlework or books. Many did voluntary work, particularly if they lived in or within striking distance of a sizeable town or a community where there was work to be done in the welfare field. In London, for example, it was common for wealthy ladies to be found actively involved in various charitable organisations in the poorer areas of the East End, or raising money for the poor or needy. In fact, on the whole, over and above society money-raising events, charitable activity was very common among the well off. Many became directly involved in a particular charity, perhaps founding a new school or medical foundation. Particularly for the ladies who had little to occupy all their time, it was an invaluable and beneficial way to divert one's energies.

The young man who left home to begin a career, very probably in business, or one of the professions or the Civil Service, would usually take lodgings in someone's house. Normally this might consist of two or three rooms. For this he might pay two guineas a week, which included breakfast every day, and various domestic services. Often a landlady would provide an evening meal as well if required, though most of their tenants always ate out.

Many families who owned large town houses in the years after the War began to find it too expensive to maintain such a large establishment. As a result many split up their homes, dividing some rooms off into small flats for their children as they reached the age where they would otherwise have moved out.

A young man arriving in London for the first time to begin work would have usually one or two introductions which would be the launching pad for his career in London society. He would call round to introduce himself to the people concerned, and hopefully, as a result, be invited to dinner. Once this foot in the door had been gained, as long as he behaved correctly and was reasonably well regarded, a single invitation could mushroom into numerous others. Normally, if a family or a particular person was to hold a large ball, the hostess would tend to use either her own or a friend's list of all those eligible young men and attractive girls who were generally regarded as being good value as guests and tended to be invited to all the best parties. All the hostesses used to compare lists, and update or add to their own as a result. So if one created a good impression with one of the London hostesses and managed to get one's name on a list, there was every likelihood of a large number of invitations. And ball invitations tended to lead to new dinner invitations, and so on.

Surprisingly, many young society ladies were never taught to dance properly, a fact which caused much annoyance to young men at balls and made those girls who did not have to be led on the floor very much more popular as partners than those who did. It was, though, rare for two young people to dance together more than a couple of times during an evening, because it was viewed as good behaviour to dance with as many people as possible, particularly with one's host or hostess, and also to be seen spending more time than was considered normal with one partner would be certain to raise eyebrows and start rumours. Discretion was the order of the day.

Dress for dinner was always either black tie or white tie — at balls and smaller dances white tie was almost invariable. In fact, a black tie was regarded as being relatively informal. In the years after the War, though, this began to change, particularly in the London clubs. Previously it would have been regarded as sacrilege not to dress for dinner in one's club but, increasingly, younger men began to rebel against this. For example, if a young man worked in the City and intended to dine at his club, it made much more sense to go straight to the club from work rather than go back to his lodgings, change and then return to the club. But this caused many raised eyebrows among the older generation. As a young businessman who joined Brooks's in 1923 recalled: 'I was ticked off more than once at the club because I didn't wear a dinner jacket for dinner every night. Once it was a friend of my father's — an ex-serviceman, a charming man and he said: "When I was a young man, nobody ever dreamed of coming into mess after seven o'clock in the evening in anything but a black tie . . .", and I replied, "Well sir, I can quite understand that, but of course we young men in the City lead a rather different life. We have our office work to do and we don't get away till six o'clock, and we get here about half-past six or seven. We dine about half-past seven and then go home. If we're to change, we've got to go home first and change, and then get a cab back here to dine. It takes up so much time, and costs far more in cab fares." But he just couldn't see it. "Oh well, when we were young . . ."'

It was normal for the young professional or businessman to dine each night at his club. Given the still high level of domestic service in middle and upper-class households, when a young man came to London he would probably have had no experience whatever of self-catering, even had there been a kitchen attached to his lodgings, which there usually was not. If the young man in question chose not to dine at his club, and he was not invited to dine elsewhere, it was normal for him to go to a favourite restaurant instead. Except for a rare meal back in digs, dining out every night was standard practice.

A young man who went into the City in the early twenties recalls on more than one occasion finding himself seated next to his hostess at a dinner party, who after a while began to question him about his family background:

'Tell me, Mr X. Isn't your mother related to Lord Y?'

'Yes, he's my uncle'.

'Oh, very nice. And how many of you are there in the family?'

'There's two boys and three girls'.

'Ah yes. And tell me, your brother, is he older, or younger . . .?'

The honest younger son soon found that he wasn't invited any more. All society mothers wanted to find a worthy elder son for their daughters to marry. Those who were cleverer lied about their families, suggesting that they were the eldest sons — it was always worth a few more dinner invitations.

Sometimes this obsession with matchmaking went to almost absurd extremes. On one occasion a young man was told by a girl whom he knew quite well that she was taking a party to a dance, but could not invite him because her mother had stipulated that all the men in the party had to be eldest sons. If the suitor was not heir to a title or to a fortune, he was not worth knowing.

Most young people lived on an allowance from their parents after leaving home, even when they might actually be in salaried employment. A normal allowance might be some £300 or £400 a year. For most this was a convenient arrangement since it meant they could afford a good lifestyle right from the start. But at a time when the young were becoming freer and more independent in all parts of society, this system only served to perpetuate the influence of parents over their children.

Marriage, for instance, was effectively impossible without the active consent of parents. Whilst there was nothing to stop a young couple eloping to some distant place to get married away from the family eye, to do so inevitably meant financial hardship. To those brought up in the affluence of upper-class life, this was usually too great a burden to bear. Parents could still veto a marriage and get away with it.

Generally the financial aspect of marriage was very important. All upper-class parents expected prospective partners for their children to come from reasonably well endowed families, and it was standard practice for the groom's family, or occasionally both, to set up the couple in their own home and to give them an allowance with which to maintain a lifestyle commensurate with parental expectations. Without that, marriage was opposed to the hilt. It was, for example, unheard-of for a society couple to begin married life with an establishment of less than three servants.

In London, if the Season was female-dominated, the clubs were the opposite extreme, totally male bastions. The central role they played in the life of the young man in London has already been seen, but they were far more than that. For men who lived outside London, the club was their home in the city, where they stayed when doing business or just passing through. It was also a place for actually doing business, where one could take an associate for lunch, or where one could simply retire to read a paper or do some overdue paperwork. It could as well be a place for political intrigue — the famous meeting of the Conservative Party in 1922 which voted to break with Lloyd George's coalition government took place in the Carlton Club in St James's. Richard Usborne, author of *Clubland Heroes*, conveys very clearly the importance of the club in a man's life: in his words, it offered him a fortress, with many of the amenities of home, but without the distractions of, or the obligations to, his womenfolk. The hall porter was a reasonable picket against all those he preferred not to meet.

Though the new upstarts in society were businessmen who, more often than not, had made money in the War, this was not to say that business was a new element in the world of the upper classes. Many of the most prominent men in prewar Britain were, as has already been mentioned, second or third generation members of commercial families. So although there were undoubtedly those who were predominantly idle, who chose to run the family estates and investments through agents despite the economic troubles of the postwar era, most had business and other interests which took up much of their time.

It was this as much as anything which tended to blur the end of the London Season. Traditionally, the coming-around of Henley and Ascot and of the summer led to a mass exodus from London, with people calling in on the major sporting events on the way back to their country houses or holidays. In fact, for many, to be found in London in August was almost sacrilegious. It was not uncommon for some people, found by friends in town during August, to state very emphatically that they were just passing through on their way to somewhere else, perhaps the Continent. Others in fact couldn't stay in London after the end of the Season simply because they had nowhere to stay, having just rented a house for its duration. Fewer and fewer people could now afford the luxury of owning a town house as well as their country seat. Sometimes men took a small house or apartment convenient for their work, or just stayed in their club.

Even so, it was becoming more and more common to find people with places in London staying there through the summer months, though female members of families tended to go to the country anyway. Men whose lives were becoming increasingly business-orientated, whose family wealth was no longer chiefly based upon land holdings, had to devote more and more of their time to managing investments or businesses. For them at least the leisured life of the old landed aristocracy was almost gone. In the past their time would have been divided between politics and pleasure. Now business was paramount.

The end of the London Season was marked by the departure of the socialite gentry to events like the Henley regatta, before they went on to their summer homes in time for the grouse season in August.

For the upper classes, the 1920s were often marked by gay social frivolities. Here young women are taught the Charleston — then sweeping the country like a plague — apparently by a Chinese.

There was still plenty of opportunity to escape the city though, even if holidays for the men were much shorter. Generally the women would set themselves up in the country for the summer, perhaps after the whole family had taken a short holiday in Europe or in Scotland. Their menfolk would return from town at weekends or perhaps for sporadic longer visits.

Away from London, society life tended to become geared to regular house parties, both planned and unplanned, for guests might telephone to invite themselves for a short time. Small groups of people would gather in the houses, for what the *Tatler* columnist Evelyn called 'unlimited tennis, golf and bridge, and a little wild dancing to the gramophone, and many opportunities for flirtations'. There was also hunting. On the 'Glorious Twelfth' of August the grouse-shooting season began, and soon after those of the other popular game birds such as woodcock, partridge, pheasant and wild duck. Soon many of the house parties would become shooting parties, and remain so through the autumn and into the winter. Others preferred fishing to hunting, and many spent long holidays in Scotland casting for trout and salmon in the rushing rivers, while the women strolled on the moors and in the forests.

Those families without London bases spent most of the rest of the year at their homes in the country — indeed many of the older generation were seldom in London if the attraction of the Season was lost on them. Society in town tended to be more the province of the young, and those without interests in London might well be infrequent visitors to the city after their early days as young people there, mixing instead with the country set. But, those who really were anyone would be back in London after the Christmas festivities to remain there through another Season.

Yet, in that last paragraph lies a clue to a point really not yet touched upon. Realistically, in a work like this one has to look upon high society as being a reasonably homogeneous entity, focussing upon London and its Season. And that analysis is far from being an inaccurate one. Yet beyond the confines of the London season there was a very definite

The Scottish season was timed to coincide with the opening of grouse shooting, the 'Glorious Twelfth' of August. Different attitudes in a grouse butt — only the gun and his loader seem to be enjoying the shooting.

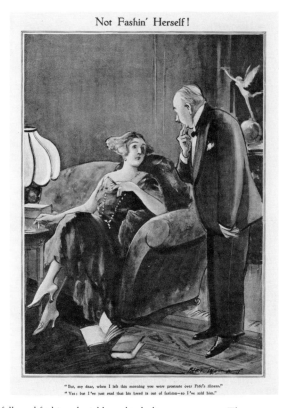

Not Fashin' Herself!

"But, my dear, when I left this morning you were prostrate over Fido's illness."
"Yes; but I've just read that his breed is out of fashion—so I've sold him."

The moneyed classes often followed fashion slavishly and to ludicrous extremes. There was much truth in this 1921 cartoon from the Sketch.

division between those who were 'in' and those who weren't. Within London itself there were more and less prominent social circles, all of which could quite properly be described as 'upper class', yet many of their members wouldn't have been invited to soirées given by the leading hostesses. Equally, out in the counties people who had been presented at court and who were seen in the Royal enclosure at Ascot earlier in the year would still dine with the vicar and hunt with the prosperous farmers when the Season was over.

Society was as much an ideal as anything else. One came from the right background or, by the twenties, one had enough money to live in a style that attracted the people who really mattered. There were acceptable forms of behaviour, things one said and things one didn't, even though these unwritten rules were being erased by the advent of the *nouveaux riches* after the War. But, even so, the society way remained very much the social ideal, emulated by middle-class social climbers throughout the country, sometimes to ridiculous extremes. For those climbers it was the ultimate goal, to be accepted by those who mattered, to be seen in the pages of the glossy magazines, really to be *someone*. And in suburban villas across England the middle classes pretended to themselves that they were on the way.

THE PUBLIC SCHOOLS

It is difficult to exaggerate the role that the English public school system has played in the history of this country over the past century. The vast majority of those who have attained high public office and positions of power and influence spent at least some of their formative years at one of the schools. They belonged, and in many ways still do belong to, a particular tradition with its own way of life and attitudes, both of which were clearly visible in the later development of most of those who attended them. But that influence spread far beyond the ranks of those who went to the schools. Public school stories filled comics and books. Characters like Billy Bunter and his companions at Greyfriars enthralled and amused boys from the worst areas. And the way of life led by even the fictional heroes of the era, Bulldog Drummond, Richard Hannay and others, all emanated from the public school way of life. It is not too much to say that the public schools made the lives of many of the most prominent Englishmen, and there are those who argue that creating such a stereotype, living life according to the ethical code instilled by public school life, has been one reason for the decline of England as a world power.

Whatever else had been changed by the First World War, the social importance of the public schools remained unchallenged, though there were one or two experiments in more progressive education at the time. The facts were simple: if you wished to have any degree of social respectability and prominence whatever, you had to send your children to public school. There could be no question of a grammar school education. That was very much a system for the middle-middle classes and below. Young people who were going to be someone went to the great public schools, to Eton, Harrow or Winchester, or to any one of numerous others. It was a social must.

But the War did not leave the public schools themselves untouched. As the years of fighting passed, so the role of honour of former pupils and members of staff grew longer. Ironically, the respect and loyalty felt by many for their former schools brought them courage and motivation in their darkest hour. Letters came from the front expressing pride at the opportunity they had been given to defend the honour of school and country. Proud they may have been, but when it was all over the memorial tablets raised in school chapels that read like past registers must have been cold comfort to those left behind.

But the way of life had to carry on, and it did, with little outward alteration. New generations of boys arrived to pursue their education, masters were demobilised and came to reclaim their old jobs. In the schools, as almost everywhere else, there was an air of levity and happiness, despite the awful losses of the fighting, just because it now really was all over.

Most of those arriving at the public schools, which they did at a variety of ages, as early as eleven up to around thirteen or perhaps even fourteen, came from the enormous number of small prep schools all over the country which provided boys and girls with the rudiments of education. It is impossible adequately to generalise about them because of the wide variety of sizes and structure of prep schools. They might be tiny establishments, with only one or two teachers and a handful of pupils, or schools of several hundred pupils. But what they all had in common was their purpose: to prepare their pupils to go on to a public school for their teenage years.

The way the academic process worked was a little less clearcut than it is today. The first thing, assuming your place had been arranged with the particular public school, was the Common Entrance examination, which everyone took at the end of their time at prep school. This was less of an entrance exam than a gauge of academic ability which enabled the public school to stream a pupil. It was normal, for example, for sons to go to the same school as their father, and indeed most public schools positively welcomed this. So, whilst the school was happy to accept a pupil, he had to be graded according to his success in the Common Entrance. Normally this was done, not by dividing each age group into classes of different ability, but rather by putting them into different school years, though, of course, under those circumstances, the term 'school year' became something of a misnomer. The fourth form could be a mix of less bright boys who had already been at the school a year or two and had gradually worked their way up, and the brightest of the Common Entrance candidates who were put at a level of teaching which they were judged to be capable of coping with. It all depended on how much teaching the school thought the pupil needed to prepare him or her for later exams.

Almost universally, the independent schools were single-sex, though a handful, notably Bedales and Dartington Hall, took both boys and girls. The result of this was that the public school mentality that did exist was very much orientated towards the one sex taught at the schools, and was reflected in some of the institutions of later life such as the gentlemen's club and the still widely practised tradition of separation after a meal when the ladies left and the men remained behind drinking port before rejoining them later.

It is common belief that the public school, both then and often still today, was a snobbish institution, epitomised by the elitism of schools like Eton, Harrow and Winchester. Yet, though it was without doubt true that many public school boys and girls were snobs outside their schools, within them the opposite was true. Firstly, and most obviously, all those who went to public school came at worst from solid and respectable family backgrounds; many were from aristocractic families or could command enormous fortunes, the social elite of British youth. Yet, though a boy might be ribbed a little if his father had a slightly doubtful or unconventional employment, his popularity depended much more on his personality and such things as his prowess on the sports field. The most popular boys were in the rugger fifteen or the cricket eleven, or were just thoroughly decent chaps. It didn't really matter whether daddy was a duke, a maharajah or just a hard-working small-town doctor who had saved carefully for his children's education.

This fact was emphasised in the continued practice in many schools of the system of fagging. Usually fagging was structured within the individual houses into which most schools were divided. The basic principle was that as a young pupil you were assigned to an older boy for whom you carried out various services. Then as you climbed up the school you ceased to be a fag and eventually were able to have a fag yourself. A Tory peer, at Eton in the 1920s, remembered that he and fellow fags cooked tea for the boys who were over

Sporting prowess was a prime consideration in boys' public schools. A scene from the 1927 cricket match between Eton and Harrow, an annual fixture of great social (although not sporting) importance to the cognoscenti.

them. They collected bread, butter, sugar and tea from the school, and cooked anything else that their seniors decided to buy to eat along with the standard fare. Whilst each fag usually worked for one elder boy, they were subject to the orders of any of the upper members of the school. If, for example, one of the older boys wanted a message carrying, he would go to the door of his room and shout 'boy' at the top of his voice. There would be pandemonium as all the fags rushed to answer the call, but it was the last to arrive who had to carry out the chore. The lucky ones were those who had rooms well placed for getting to the rooms of the older boys in a hurry.

To those who never attended a public school, and indeed probably to many who did, the system may seem unusual, and perhaps unnecessary. However, the view of those who did approve of it was that, particularly in a school like Eton where many of the pupils went on to reach prominent positions, and all achieved sufficient wealth and standing to have staff and employees of their own, it was a very good thing to gain some experience of what it was like to have to obey orders.

Eton was — and still is — unusual in that it provided all of its pupils with their own room, a retreat which could be decorated as one's own and in which one could have some degree of privacy. Each room had its own fire, which was allowed to be lit during winter, which again provided a degree of comfort and individuality. At most schools this simply didn't happen. All the younger boys slept in dormitories, and only as a pupil progressed up the school was there any chance of getting one's own — or even a shared — study or room.

Most schools were actually ruled by their sixth forms. The teaching staff and house-masters were there for academic purposes and to oversee and generally they left law and

Eton College was then — as it still is today — regarded by most people as the acme of public schools. The uniform was already antiquated, even by the 1920s, but had the one merit of being, unlike many, reasonably comfortable.

order to the prefects and the older boys. Though at first this seems unusual, it was an intricate part of the public school system, which was designed to initiate the young into the respectable and carefully ordered ways of their parents. This was one of the few facets of society as a whole which was strengthened rather than changed by the War. Within the schools, masters and headmasters who had suffered the anguish of ever-lengthening rolls of honour saw the victory of 1918 as a justification of the system that their schools sought to uphold. It had been a long fight, but they had won through in the end. Furthermore, the wartime economy had brought the *nouveaux riches* to London and provincial society. The men who had made their fortune building dreadnoughts and tanks and bullets wanted their sons to be brought up as gentlemen, and the public schools were the obvious means to this end.

In fact the fagging system was a very good way of ensuring that the disciplinary hierarchy in the schools ran smoothly and under its own steam. Any boy who suffered the hardships of the system, being educated while acting as servant for an older boy, did so secure in the knowledge that one day he would enjoy the power that was now being exerted over him.

Away from the classroom, the schools were enormously hierarchical. Boys fought hard to achieve small status gains, such as moving up a form, something that was not by any means automatic at the end of a year, and winning sporting colours and caps. Once achieved, privileges were enforced very firmly. Many who had been treated badly as fags behaved with equal harshness towards their own fags in later years. Others were able to learn the lessons of their past, and treat their successors more fairly, but still very much according to the rules of the system.

Many schools had initiation ceremonies for the youngest arrivals. These had often, during the nineteenth century, been brutal, and although by the twenties this was no longer true, some were humiliating enough for a nervous young boy in his early days at a large and daunting new school. At Marlborough, for example, new boys had to crawl along a red-hot radiator singing 'Clementine' and at the end were slapped on the face.

Even beatings for misdemeanours were the province of the upper end of the school hierarchy. The guilty were letting down the honour of the school, something which as one rose up the school and achieved status and privilege, became more and more important. Even those further up the school were subject to the discipline of the prefects and could be beaten for stepping out of line.

As mentioned, sporting ability very much affected the degree to which one could hope to rise up the school hierarchy as one grew older, and conditioned the way in which others viewed you. That could mean the difference between popularity and unpopularity, and one's happiness or unhappiness at school. Many were the boys who led undistinguished and unpopular lives for years, and then discovered some latent sporting talent which got them into one of the school teams. Suddenly they were on the school map, and became one of the chaps. It may sound harsh on those who were inept at sport, but often that inability could ruin their schooldays. At Lancing in 1920, for example, those who were failures at sport were contemptible, and known in the schools as 'wrecks'.

The sports themselves reflected the honour and codes of the system. It is undoubtedly from this origin that the expression 'It's not cricket' as a statement of honour comes. On the field everyone was expected to play fair and act according to the rules, as well as to the style book. It was far better in a game of cricket to play an elegant shot which failed to get runs than to slog the ball for six, though of course the player who could combine the two was a school hero.

One reason, perhaps, for the high profile of games in the public schools may have been the tedium of the classroom. Because so much of future academic prospects still depended on classics, they were taught at enormous length. Without success in them, it was difficult to get into Oxford or Cambridge, even in an era where academic prowess was less important than today in securing a place at the two universities. Of course there were ways round this. A man who had distinguished himself at school could almost certainly find his way into Oxbridge without too much academic success. But the schools couldn't prepare everyone for the sporting path to university, so the classics had to be studied at length. And the sports field was a welcome relief for many from hours of verbs and declensions.

Indeed for most pupils and some members of the school authorities the public schools weren't really academic institutions at all. They were places to groom a new generation of English gentlemen, versed in the knowledge of how to behave, dress and conduct their lives in general. Many could see nowhere more appropriate for this to take place than on the cricket or rugby field. There boys could participate as teams, learn the rules and play by them, and play as amateurs, who enjoyed themselves and played hard, but took adversity in their stride. Some boys stayed on at school for a term or two when they could have left, and parents paid their fees just so that they could continue to contribute their sporting talent to the school. The same was true of those offered a place at the top of the school hierarchy, perhaps the chance to be head boy or a prefect. Matches between the great schools were recorded in detail by the press and followed eagerly by old boys who always retained an interest in the old school and how it was doing.

In fact, sporting prowess at school could make one's reputation for years to come. The writer T.C. Worsley, for example, found his success on the cricket field paying dividends years after in the early 1930s, when he submitted a single poem to the *London Mercury*, which was accepted, and received an invitation to drop in on the editor sometime. When he eventually did so, the following conversation (quoted in Jonathan Gathorne Hardy's *The Public School Phenomenon*) took place:

'What did you say your name was?'

'Worsley'

'And the initials?'

'T.C.'

He tried them over several times: T.C. Worsley, T.C. Worsley: and then something clicked.

'Not *the* T.C. Worsley?'

Heavens! Was I so well known already? If so, how had it come about? I had published nothing but this one sonnet in his magazine. Did this make me *the* T.C. Worsley? How amazing! Was it as good as that? No it wasn't, as his next question showed.

'Let me see, Let me see,' he rummaged through his memory. 'I've got it. Marlborough *v* Rugby at Lords three years running. Forty-three in the second innings of the second year. Perambulators against Etceteras, eighty-two. Fenners, 1929. University *v* Yorkshire same year. Am I right?'

He was, to within a run or two, and was delighted to be told so. 'There you are. Of course I'll publish your poems. Leave them with us.'

Such was the influence of sport and the old school tie.

There were those who saw sport as a vital part of school life if only because it diverted sexual energies away from possible homosexuality. That was rife in the public schools, even though it was looked upon with horror by the authorities who strove to make sure it didn't take place. It was thought that any boy who had any spare time at all would get into sexual mischief, and the games field and the rewards for persistent effort and success were one way of depriving them of leisure.

But homosexuality there was, not because the boys who went to the public schools were statistically any more likely to be homosexuals, but because they passed much of their adolescent and pubescent development in the confines of a single-sex establishment. Their exposure to girls was minimal for much of the time. So most young sexual attachments were between members of the same sex. And given that the majority of teenage boys are sexually active by the age of fifteen or sixteen, at least in terms of masturbation, made it certain that many of these schoolboy attractions for members of the same sex would have a physical side to them.

But the penalties were severe: being caught in a compromising position with another boy meant the embarrassment of certain expulsion and the shame brought to one's parents in an era where many were still very naive sexually. In the early thirties, for example, when Lord Beauchamp was exposed as a homosexual, his wife didn't even know what the word meant.

Those whose early passions were actively physical had, therefore, to resort to subterfuge and guile to beat the eagle eye of staff and the prefects at the top of the school. Some resorted to cutting holes in each others' trouser pockets, so that they could withdraw their hands hurriedly if caught. But for many the penalties, and the efforts of the school authorities to make sure that nothing did take place, ensured such attachments came to nothing. Instead they were expressed, and perhaps not even recognised, by glances across a dormitory, and boys only found physical release from them through masturbation.

In fact, the efforts of the authorities to stamp out homosexuality often went to ridiculous lengths. At Malvern the lavatories had no doors; at Stowe the seats in chapel were arranged so that they didn't face each other and boys could not exchange passionate glances. At many schools acting was discouraged because the authorities feared it might lead to sex. And timetabling was rigid. Boys would know exactly what they would be doing for weeks ahead, and they would always be doing something. In this way the authorites minimised free time, tried to divert sexual energies through sport, kept different age groups and houses apart as much as possible — except obviously for fagging — and generally did their best to ensure that as few boys as possible ever came to the point where they had to pack their trunk and return home in disgrace.

By contrast, even with the general decline in religion, church played a very prominent part in school life. Chapel on Sunday was a strict part of the timetable, but the links between the staff and the church were even more noticeable. Many of those who held the major headmasterships had clerical backgrounds — in the nineteenth century most had. As late as the inter-war years it was still very likely that the headmaster of Eton, and his counterparts at the other major public schools could, if they wished, continue their clerical career, perhaps becoming a bishop or a dean. This was, of course, changing along with the decline in religious attendance generally, but even so the links were still strong. Many schools were only now beginning to appoint non-churchmen to their top jobs, and the influence of the Church was still strong.

Even as late as the 1920s, the public school curriculum was dominated by the classics, and particularly Latin. Every school had numerous classics masters, though seldom as many as they had had a century earlier, when in most schools the classics teachers out-numbered all the rest. Latin was essential to getting a university place, and the highest academic honour attainable was certainly a first in Classics.

But the curriculum had broadened greatly since the middle of the nineteenth century. Then, classics masters had looked upon others as inferiors, and few schools offered much teaching in other subjects. But that had changed by the turn of the century, and by the 1920s a curriculum consisting of English — both language and literature — history, geography, French, maths and science was the norm. Even so, a school like Winchester didn't have a proper English department until the 1960s. Classics remained very much the most important part of the schooling of most boys.

For the public schoolboy, access to university was relatively easy — he had only to pass the university exam, or to secure five school certificate passes. The standard was low because it was designed to admit those who weren't able enough to pass an honours degree, but who could muddle through an ordinary degree and contribute to the university life and to the college's achievements on the sports field.

For those who didn't have the automatic launching pad in life that an Oxbridge place provided, the old school tie could be just as effective. There were always family firms or friends of father to go to work for. And there were still good entrées into the military or to the Empire even for those who didn't make it to university. But most did, and a new future beckoned, though still one which in many ways reflected the standards and the upbringing of the public school world they were leaving.

So far, little mention has been made of the girls' public schools, of which there were many though far fewer in number than their male equivalents. Though they were in many ways very similar, differences did exist, and because of that it is easier to deal with them separately.

The most clearcut difference was that in the girls' schools a far greater emphasis was placed upon the education itself. There was no alternative route to prowess, as the boys had on the sports field. In an uneven world, the girls' schools had to strive hard to give their pupils an education which could match that provided for boys. Though the War had brought the role of women to the forefront much more than had been the case beforehand, society still did not as a whole expect its women to be as talented or to achieve as much as the men.

Because there were far fewer places at university for girls, far more effort had to be put into preparation for the Oxford and Cambridge exams. They put very heavy pressure on the girls as a result, and competition for the places that there were was intense. In part this was because many of the ladies who rose to prominent positions on the staff of the girl's schools were totally dedicated to their work, and strove to prove that women could do just as well as men. But this desire was not universal, and many schools offered lessons for life with almost as much emphasis as academic lessons.

Over and above the normal academic subjects there were parts of the curriculum of many schools which recognised the fact that much of what they were doing was a waste of time. Few of the facts and skills learned at school would ever be used, since most of the girls would end up as wives and mothers. So many schools ran, alongside compulsory games as non-academic activities, lessons which prepared the girls for the future that they were most likely to have. Among others, there were lessons in domestic science, bridge and wine tasting. These things would probably be of far more use to them in the future than the classics, though they were taught this as much as the boys.

The result of this emphasis both on academic prowess and preparation for a more domestic future meant excessively long working days for many girls away at school, some-

In girls' public schools, too, sports loomed large in the curriculum. Few, however, attempted cricket, although Roedean did, as this early 1930s photograph shows.

124

times from as early as six or seven in the morning through virtually non-stop to around nine at night.

This meant that games were a far less important part of the intensive day than at the boys' schools. This is not to say *un*important — in some girls' schools, most notably Roedean, sporting prowess was of great importance — but the emphasis seems to have been more on doing well academically, and proving that girls could be good at games too, rather than on sport as a means of education in its own right. There can also be no doubt that the interest in sport in schools like Roedean was at least in part influenced by the fact that sport was such a dominating presence in the boys' schools. In other words, the same girls who were pushed as hard as possible in their studies to enable them to emulate the academic careers of their brothers, were pushed into attempting to emulate them on the sports field as well.

Certainly there was a far more actively competitive spirit in girls' sport, in the hockey and lacrosse tournaments in which they played. The men were taught to be competitive, but good competitors at the same time. It wasn't that the girls were meant to be any different, but there does seem to have been more emphasis on actually winning the cup at the end of the day. It was, for many, as important as playing for the sake of it.

Discipline in the girls' public school was rigid, even more so than in their male counterparts. Contact with men was totally outlawed in most schools, with the exception of fathers, brothers, and perhaps a token male music teacher. A pupil at Cheltenham in the early twenties remembers that when the girls went out for walks in long lines, crocodiles as they were and still are nicknamed, and they came across boys from the local all-male public school, they had to avert their eyes and pass on the other side of the road. Various parts of the town were also strictly out of bounds, and the area around the boys' school doubly so.

In fact most of the girls thought this to be extraordinary, since few had any real desire to meet up with the boys anyway. Particularly among the younger girls, they were regarded as spotty, immature and altogether rather undesirable. Yet still the staff persisted in trying to protect their girls from the imagined evils of contact with men, going to lengths that even surpassed the campaign against homosexuality waged in the boys' schools. In the 1930s a member of staff at Roedean discovered that parts of the school grounds were visible from the upper floor of passing double decker buses. There was immediate panic among the staff, and vast wooden barricades were erected within a week to shut off the view. No man could be allowed to see, and perhaps be tempted by, a Roedean girl.

But, despite the enclosed environment, unlike the boys' schools, there was little sexuality among the girls, at least not in the physical sense. It was, though, very fashionable to have a 'pash' or a crush on one of the older girls. Love between pupils, whether requited or not, could be just as strong as it was amongst the boys, but it tended to be rather more remote and less seldom expressed. The boys did actually develop relationships with one another; girls were more likely to idolise and fantasise from afar.

Interestingly, though the girls' public school mentality grew up alongside that of the boys', and their gentlemen's code, the two were markedly dissimilar. Whereas heroes like Bulldog Drummond came to epitomise the way a chap should behave, the girls' heroines were more slapdash, rather the St Trinians type on a more sensible level: theirs was the world of 'Jolly Hockey Sticks' and all that.

Their world was also much more artistic, something which in itself added something to the atmosphere of the school. Girls were positively encouraged to get involved in theatrical productions, and at Cheltenham there used to be fierce rivalry between the different houses to see who could put on the best end of year or end of term play.

Inter-house rivalry was in fact probably much stronger than in the boys' schools. Cheltenham had separate uniforms for its various houses, and the younger girls were not allowed to talk to people from other houses, a rule which caused much anguish to new girls seeking directions and unable to find a member of their own house to consult.

In a sense it all came down to the idea of beating the men. The whole atmosphere of the schools was geared to competition. Exam time was a great strain because so much was expected of you. On the sports field you had to play hard and play fair, and win as well; that was just as important.

Whether due to this, or to ability alone, many of the girls who went on to university were every bit as well educated and prepared for life as their male counterparts. Aged seventeen or eighteen, girls returned home to do voluntary work while they waited to get married, or they went to a finishing school to fill in time before returning home to do the same. But more and more were going on to continue their education. For the majority that continuation was to be within the hallowed confines of Britain's two most distinguished universities.

OXBRIDGE

Oxford and Cambridge have always been the bastions of English academia, and were always highly select socially. Indeed only in recent years have they begun to become less exclusive, accepting young people not just from the middle and upper class elite but from all backgrounds. Rules have become more liberal — today's student can behave in a manner his predecessors would never have dreamed of. But at the same time many of the oldest and best known Oxbridge traditions have faded as a result. And there can be no doubt that the beginnings of the liberalisation of the two universities lay, as in so many other aspects of the lives of the young in England, in the impact of the First World War and its aftermath.

Edwardian Oxbridge had been a place vastly different to that of today. There were far fewer undergraduates in each college, perhaps only one fifth or even less of the number to be found studying there now. A college with some three hundred students today might well have had less than fifty before the First World War. The subjects studied were somewhat limited and more traditional in nature. For example Classics was perhaps the most highly recognised of all courses, and many of the great figures of the era were Oxford and Cambridge classics scholars.

Rules were entirely different from those of today. The attitude to relations between men and women was such that Cambridge's only girls' colleges, Girton and Newnham, were built away from the centre of the town. College curfews were universal and punishments for failing to keep the rules were severe, often even going so far as to send down students from the university for offences which today would probably not warrant much more than a brief lecture.

But the outbreak of the First World War had a profound effect upon the two universities. If the flower of English youth died in Flanders, then so did the flower of Oxbridge. Both universities lost some 2,000 students, dons and college employees fighting side-by-side for their country. For four years much of the academic work of the college was abandoned. Some opened their doors to servicemen, either to provide medical and recuperative facilities for wounded men or, later in the War, to provide billeting for Americans on their way to the conflict. A few undergraduates remained, but the majority of colleges effectively closed down until 1918.

As soon as demobilisation began the soldiers started to come back to take up their studies where they had been left off. Perhaps surprisingly, few found the sudden reversion in their lifestyle hard to adjust to. Most resumed their academic work with a renewed zeal, almost as if they were trying to catch up with the time they had lost. And indeed that is almost certainly exactly what they felt. While the majority of the men who had been away to the War and returned safely were from humble backgrounds and saw the army as a great escape from the drudgery of their working lives, a young undergraduate whose husband was one of those who came back to restart their studies, recalled that he and his friends had a genuine regret for the time lost and felt an urgent need to avoid wasting any more of their lives. And so they worked, perhaps as hard as they had ever done, though not entirely at the expense of enjoyment and leisure.

But there were those for whom the return in 1918 or 1919 to the colleges where they had been what probably seemed an age earlier was as much a release as anything. As the youth of the country danced its nights away, as gaiety dispersed what had seemed an interminable nightmare, so some of the returning undergraduates took to university social life with a similar zeal. Few tried to keep the events of the past four years in the forefront of their intellectual discussions. Instead they talked of love, merrymaking and more and more about the previously taboo subject of intimacy between the sexes.

For the new generations of undergraduates, too young to have fought in the War, it was a difficult time to be embarking upon their university lives. They tended to feel ill-at-ease alongside men who had risen to senior army positions at an age that would have been inconceivable in peacetime and who had now returned to finish their interrupted education. Some of the younger arrivals flourished in this rather awkward environment, but it was not always a happy mix.

Although the years after the War were very much ones of transition in the attitudes of the young, Oxbridge and its students still retained a strong streak of conservatism, a lack of rebelliousness. One reason for this is perhaps the degree of college loyalty that existed at the time. Most of a student's social life and particular pastimes took place within his own college. And both on the sports field and elsewhere there was far more inter-college rivalry than there is today. Young men had an almost emotional attachment to their college — in those days it would be normal for someone to say 'I was at Balliol' rather than 'I was at Oxford'. Today that seldom happens.

Furthermore, the vast majority of Oxbridge students — indeed virtually all — came from the public school system, where discipline and tradition had been hammered into them from the youngest age. It was not that they did not question rules, but most believed strongly in their university and would not have contemplated seriously challenging it; academic dress was of course compulsory at various times of the day and in various places. For the age of Oxbridge discipline was far from over.

This strength of feeling for the college was not just to be found among the students, but also among all those who worked in it, whether dons or college servants. The dons were in college far more than is the case today where, for some at least, the job is little more than a normal nine-to-five one and at the end of the day they return to wives and families somewhere out of town. But in the twenties this was rarely the case: the majority of dons dined in college each night, returning to their homes much later in the evening. Many who were not married lived in the college — indeed it was rare for any of them to move outside unless they were married.

Dons' wives were seldom seen in college, except on a Sunday evening when chapel attendance was pretty well compulsory, certainly for students and effectively for their teachers as well. Then all would congregate for a service, but afterwards the husbands and wives would separate — the men to dine in Hall with the head of their college, the women to return home or eat together somewhere. College, with its strict segregationist and anti-

Most university colleges still had a strong sporting tradition, and inter-college competition could be fierce. For Oxford and Cambridge, however, the University Boat Race was the high point of an oarsman's ambitions. Cambridge Trial Eights, at the end of a race, December 1922.

In the 'old universities' academic dress for undergraduates was compulsory much of the time. Undergraduates on the steps of Queen's College, Oxford, in the 1930s.

feminist traditions, was sacrosanct, and was paramount in the life of a don, and essentially took precedence over his private life.

This shared sense of pride in the individual college generally created a very good relationship between dons and students. The former were very interested in undergraduate activities, particularly in such things as sport where prowess on the river or on the cricket pitch meant so much to the communal college pride. Because there were far fewer students than there are today everyone tended to know everyone else, even to the point of social-ising together. Often friendships were formed between younger dons and their pupils which outlasted university days.

Most students came up to Oxford or Cambridge around the age of eighteen and though some would live in college for part of their time there, the majority spent most of their academic lives living in digs, normally in private houses around the town with busy and hardworking, yet often strict, landladies. There was a much greater degree of personal service within the college than is the case today. Most university students today still enjoy some form of cleaning service, but nowhere is it on the scale of the past. The Scout or Gyp as the cleaning lady/personal servant was and is known, would bring the student breakfast, light and keep up his fire, do all his cleaning, even of such things as shoes, and generally keep the room in order. Out in digs most landladies provided a similar kind of service.

Parties could also be held in rooms and, for a charge, meals served there, waited on by college staff. Indeed this was one of the standard forms of entertaining for many students, assuming that they could afford it. Most had little problem in doing so.

The college servants more often than not knew every one of the students up at their college at any one time, and those who had been there for years past. An old college member visiting could always be certain of friendly recognition from most of the staff. And relations between staff and students was anything but that of master and servant. Most staff regarded undergraduates with a degree of what was almost affection and pride, while they themselves were regarded by both dons and students with some degree of respect, almost as institutions. Relations were perhaps rather similar to that which has always existed in the British army between officers and NCOs. It was a stark contrast to the situation elsewhere. In Oxford and Cambridge nobody minded being a college servant. But, in the outside world, fewer and fewer people were prepared to go into other forms of service.

In reality, undergraduates then were very little different to their successors today. They enjoyed much the same things and found time for as much work as play. Even so, university regulations did make life far more restricted than it has now become. The university policemen, called proctors, and their assistants, known as bulldogs, were constantly out patrolling the streets, stopping students for not wearing the correct academic dress (compulsory in many places and at certain times of the day) or for being out at illegal hours. All colleges had very strict gate hours, some shutting for the night as early as nine o'clock.

Of course there were ways round these restrictions. Every college had its own ways of climbing back in after hours, and the less cautious could get away with this. There was also, in the postwar era, a realisation on the part of college and university authorities that the men who had come back from the War could not be treated in quite the same way as they had been before. Porters were less inclined to lie in wait to catch latecomers as they climbed back over the wall, although there were, of course, still some who took great delight in doing so. Proctors were not always as severe as they might once have been. But these were cosmetic changes. The reality was that university discipline remained little changed, perhaps because so many people regarded it as being an almost sacrosanct part of the tradition on which the university was founded.

One issue, though, would not go away. Before the First World War contact between the sexes had been strictly regimented within the confines of the university, and given as little encouragement as possible. This was particularly true of the women's colleges. The rather antiquated rules at Newnham in Cambridge, for example, decreed that no girl was allowed either to visit or be visited by a man in either one's room unless a married lady was present there as a chaperone. But, to the consternation of less well-off students, any girl who was sufficiently rich to allow her to afford a suite of rooms in the college was allowed to entertain men in her sitting room. It seemed that the sight of a bed present in the same room would prove too much for any young couple to resist.

So the courting couple had to resort to subterfuge, unless they could find a better excuse to meet or had the audacity of the young Frances Partridge, later one of the Bloomsbury set, who was at Newnham after the War. She invented a chaperone for the benefit of the college authorities. A common interest such as music could provide a good reason for meeting. One couple from Oxford met regularly at meetings of the Bach Choir there. And it was possible to sneak away for a pleasant afternoon stroll alongside the Cam or the Cherwell.

But the question of the place of women in a still male-dominated university was far more involved than simply one of how and where they could meet men. At the end of the War, even though there were womens' colleges at both universities and students from both sexes sat the same examinations, women still had not been granted full membership of the two universities, and although awarded degrees at the end of the course, women could not use the titles which those degrees had given them. The result was, at both undergraduate and college levels, that the question of the female university presence became one of the most dominant issues of the era. The realities of the War and the changes that it had brought had effectively sounded the death knell of Oxford and Cambridge as male bastions. It was to be many years before the liberalisation process and the feminisation would be seen to make a clear impact, but the first few years after the War saw the beginning of the end of the old ways.

The first casualty was the code of conduct for meetings between male and female students. Even traditional Oxbridge was not totally immune to the new mood of the twenties, despite retaining much of its rigidity. Young people wanted to dance, socialise and make merry and as the War generation passed on to other things to be replaced by a new public school intake so the rush to work and make up for lost time faded. There was no great rebellion against the old ways, with issues such as free love more discussed intellectually than practised. Students still worked and played hard for their colleges, but even so they wanted to enjoy themselves. And mixed company was restricted by antiquated rules.

Very soon after the end of the War the college authorities bowed to the inevitable, though their concessions were modest. No one was prevented from entertaining a member of the opposite sex, but they could only do so at certain times, and certainly not later in the evening. In many colleges it was strictly forbidden to be seen with a girl after a certain time of night. At least though, the age of the chaperone was gone.

It took a very short time for Oxford to banish the absurd status of women as undergraduates within the university. In 1920 the university authorities passed, almost without dissent, a change to its statutes which admitted women to full membership and the right actually to use the degree titles that they had earned. But Cambridge was not so ready for change. There the issue aroused great controversy and, despite a long campaign by more progressive dons to bring a similar sense of realism to this university, it was not to be. Some concessions were made, but they fell well short of giving women the same status as men. Indeed it was not until a full twenty-five years later that Cambridge finally accepted reality and conceded female membership.

Much more than today, Oxford and Cambridge in the twenties still provided the backbone of the British Civil Service, politicians and professionals, diplomats and often sportsmen. The competition provided today by other universities did not exist on the same scale then. Of course there were other universities, but in reality ex-students say that most tended to be little more than part-residential technical colleges. Whilst sharing some of the facilities and courses offered by the two oldest universities, they had little of the same community spirit, and the old-boy nostalgia which went with former Oxbridge students for a lifetime. To some extent this was due to the part-residential nature of many of the other colleges and universities. Young men often commuted from their parents' home to the university in the nearest large town or city, attended lectures or tutorials and then caught the train home again. They had little contact with those who lived on the university campus, and knew little of what went on outside the immediate world of their faculties. It was not a situation conducive to creating a college spirit and a university identity of the kind to be found in Oxbridge.

By 1921 many of the survivors of the lost generation had gone from Oxbridge, and moved on to careers which they had been eager to take up as soon as they could finish their degrees. Those that remained were nearing the end of their time. Gradually the two universities, with the annual inflow of new students from the public schools, were returning to some semblance of normality. Soon everyone would be the same age, sharing the same experiences and the same naive innocence that those who had come back from the War had lost in the trenches or working with the wounded.

But nothing would really be the same again. The age-old conventions in university regulations and practice had been shaken and would, as the years passed, continue slowly to crumble. Though the new generation had not experienced the horrors of the War, its impact had nonetheless rubbed off on them as well. Conventions lifted for the adults who came back could not be reimposed for the children that followed. The long process of modernisation, the revolution that brought the mixed and relatively rule-free student world of today, had begun.

THE SERVANT PROBLEM

In the first quarter of this century everybody who was anybody had servants, and as everybody wanted to be anybody, even those who couldn't really afford it still employed a maid or two to maintain some semblance of grandeur — even if, when compared with the huge establishments still maintained by the wealthy aristocracy, it was a fairly paltry grandeur.

Still, servants, whether one or many, were still essential to any status on the social ladder, though those who could afford to keep half-a-dozen servants tended to look down on those who had only one. If one was to dine formally and in style; if, as etiquette and pride demanded, the home was to be perpetually immaculate, then one could not do without domestic service.

But the years after the War were not the same as those that had gone before it, even though few wealthy employers of servants realised it in 1918. As in so many parts of British society, the world of 1914 was anything but gone, and in the homes of the wealthy most servants lived much as before. Yet, increasingly, the views of the younger generation which had always filled the bulk of domestic service positions were changing. Working as 'skivvies' for others did not fit with a growing mood of independence among the young.

There can be no question but that the life of most domestic servants — even as late as the 1920s — was one of drudgery and toil, with little leisure and virtually no independence. It was a very isolated existence and, depending on the size of establishment, could also be very lonely. Indeed this latter point is most important. There is perhaps a tendency to regard the history of domestic service with some degree of uniformity. Nothing could be further from the truth. With the obvious exception of the simple nature of individual chores, a life in service in a large house with a large staff bore little relation to that of one or two staff living and working in a much smaller middle-class home.

Servants' quarters were strictly separate from the main part of the house occupied by the family. In the Victorian era this had become a fundamental part of the design of middle-class as well as upper-class homes. Servants worked in the basement, and lived in the attic. To ensure that in passing between these two points they did not disturb the harmony of the household, many houses incorporated a back staircase, usually unlit and uncarpeted, giving the servants access to their cramped living quarters above.

The attic rooms were generally spartan, to say the least. Servants slept two, three, or occasionally even four to a room, often still sharing a bed. The walls were generally drab and unpainted, floorboards were bare, the beds consisted of old iron bedsteads with lumpy

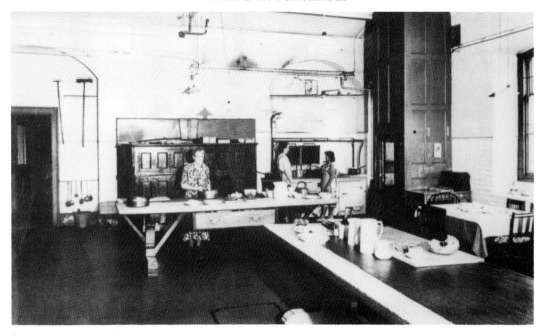

Servants were a fact of life and taken for granted even in lower-middle-class households. Their quarters, certainly in larger houses, were kept strictly separate, and their world revolved around the 'servants' hall', which was often the kitchen.

mattresses. Most of the furniture tended to be oddments which members of the family downstairs no longer wanted.

Even when a house had been modernised with gas or electrical fittings, there were many employers who deemed the expense of installing such mod cons in the servants' rooms unnecessary. Many were still lit by candles, and it was not uncommon on a winter's morning for the servants to find their water jugs and even their facecloths frozen solid.

Sometimes, though, even a spartan attic room was almost luxurious. Young men, in particular, often had to sleep in odd places around the house, perhaps on a bed in the servants' hall which could only be let down when all else was finished. Butlers often slept by the safe in their small pantry in large establishments where the contents were sufficiently valuable to give cause for concern.

Servants' bathrooms were not common, though by the twenties they were becoming less rare. Often the servants were expected to bathe in tubs, or out in the wash house, in the hot water which had been used to do the linen beforehand. Those servants' bathrooms that there were tended to be made up of cast-offs — an old iron bath and a chipped basin, for example. In any case baths were not encouraged — once a week was normally quite enough for any servant, and then on his or her day off.

During the day, though obviously there was work to be done around the house, the central base for all the servants was what was often inaptly named the servants' hall. In many places the servants' hall and the kitchen were one and the same thing, and if there was a separate sitting room for the servants, it was normally anything but large.

Generally, depending upon the size of house, the basement area, which was the principal domain of the staff, consisted of this kitchen and general servants' area, together with a number of storerooms, including a larder and a coal cellar, and perhaps a butler's pantry or a small room for the housekeeper. In this downstairs world there was a degree of hierarchy and demarcation every bit as clear as that which existed in the society upstairs. Furthermore, there was sometimes a degree of relative status even between those who did similar jobs, but who worked up in the house, rather than being confined to the servants' area.

At the top of this domestic pecking order was either the housekeeper or the butler, but again this did depend very much upon the wealth of the individual employer. If there were menservants other than the butler — and frequently there weren't — these would normally be footmen, and perhaps a houseboy who did odd jobs as well. In some large houses, though, there were a number of butlers, dividing work between them, perhaps with individual responsibility for something like wine.

The housekeeper, apart from being the most senior female servant, was also head of the whole establishment in all but the largest homes, where there might also be a steward. Normally, though, this was only the case on the country estates. Beneath the housekeeper came the cook, and then numerous ranks of maids doing varying tasks.

Actual numbers of servants employed did vary very much and many middle-class houses, though reasonably prosperous, made do with only a very small number, perhaps only a cook and a couple of maids.

Though there might be more senior servants, it was normally the cook who ruled the servants' hall, even those over whom she had no direct sway. Indeed it was not uncommon in Victorian times for cooks to strike terror into the hearts even of their employers. How far, by the twenties, the old myth of the ferocious cook was still generally true is a little doubtful. What is certain, though, is that there were plenty of old harridans still around preparing vast dinners and terrifying those who worked with them.

Not all servants worked indoors — the Earl of Ellesmere's chauffeurs at the time of the First World War. Drivers were much in demand during the war, and few chauffeurs were able to escape military service.

It was not unknown for a cook in one of the larger houses to refuse to mix with the other servants; instead she had her own room off the servants' hall where she might be waited on by the kitchen maid. Certainly she, along with the butler and housekeeper, had to be treated by the other servants virtually as they would the gentry. The butler and housekeeper were always addressed as 'Sir' and 'Madam', and cook was always 'Mrs' regardless of her marital status. Furthermore, a senior servant should only be spoken to if he or she spoke first, and at meals in the servants' hall only the housekeeper at one end of the table and the butler at the other were ever allowed to speak.

But the vast majority of domestic servants were young people, often as young as thirteen or fourteen, frequently pressed into service by parents unable to afford the size of their families, and keen to push the eldest into employment as soon as possible. Boys were less of a problem until unemployment began to bite after the 1921 depression began; there was always the local pit or mill. But even though job opportunities for girls were vastly increased after 1918, for many there was little real alternative to a life in service. From these came the vast ranks of kitchen maids, tweenies or between maids, and the less frequent male presence in the form of the bootboys. It was the maids who did most of the household cleaning, rising at the crack of dawn and working solidly throughout the day with little time to rest. The tendency of the majority of the prosperous classes to enjoy a late dinner, with the exception of the northern millowners who preferred 'high tea', meant that there was little respite until late on into the evenings.

The rambling nature of many old houses also tended to exacerbate the workload. Where there was as yet no electricity, there were oil lamps to be trimmed and lit. Fires had to be lit and kept up in every room. Beds had to be made and rooms cleaned. Some employers drew up strict rotas of work for individual servants, and those that survive show quite how much there was for a young girl to do. This example of a parlourmaid's chores is from a house in Somerset in the early twenties, quoted in *Not In Front of The Servants* by Frank Victore Dawes:

PARLOURMAID

To be downstairs at 6.30 a.m. Summer
6.45 a.m. Winter

Open shutters first.
Do Dining Room fire, and dust room.
Lay breakfast by 8.15 a.m.
Dust Hall and stairs, Morning Room and Drawing Room.
After own breakfast clear Dining Room breakfast.
Help make beds. Make own bed.

Mondays:	Trim lamps. Help given with cleaning lamp chimneys. Wash glass and silver. Clean Drawing Room and grate. Lay fire.
Tuesdays:	Clean Dining Room silver. Afternoon: own day off.
Wednesdays:	1st week — clean Dining Room. 2nd week — clean Hall and polish brass and oak. 3rd week — clean extra silver.
Thursdays:	Clean and polish silver.

Fridays: Clean Parlourmaid's Pantry.

Saturdays: Clean Morning Room and China Pantry. Dust stairs and Dining Room after lunch.

Sundays: Light Drawing Room fire if needed. Alternate Sundays: get Afternoon Tea and wash up. Lay supper table. Time off after 6 p.m. or 2 p.m. on alternate Sundays.

Generally: Answer front door. Wait at meals, clear and wash up. Bring in coal and logs as needed. To be in by 10 p.m. on days off.

In the same household the housemaid, who had a similarly heavy workload, was also expected to spend every afternoon until 7 p.m. sewing.

Of course, the amount to be done each day did vary tremendously, according to what the 'family' was doing. If, for example, there was a large dinner party or an 'At Home', then the day would inevitably be more hectic than ever.

Probably the hardest worked and longest suffering of all the servants was the kitchen maid or scullery maid, who had not even the relative pleasure of at least working in the luxurious surroundings of a grand house. The kitchen and the servants' hall were usually drab, the work was hard and having the cook as an immediate superior could be a nightmare.

Despite the more 'progressive' nature of a girl's dress throughout society after the War, those in service were still expected to dress plainly, normally in a set uniform prescribed by their employers which they had to buy out of their own relatively meagre incomes. Often, before a young girl entered service her family had to scrimp and save, even borrowing money from relatives to enable her to buy the uniform which would enable her to begin her new job. Without it she was unemployable. In fact, menservants tended to be provided with their uniforms by employers, frequently because a household retained traditional liveried uniforms for footmen and other menservants such as chauffeurs. This, though, was certainly more common in stately homes than elsewhere.

But for the girls the uniform was a perpetual problem. There could be little question of replacing worn-out clothing regularly out of their meagre wages. Instead, many hours were spent darning, patching and mending. And the wages *were* still meagre, on the whole, though the real income of the more senior servants did begin to rise quite fast towards the end of the War and continued to do so on into the twenties. By the mid-twenties a cook might earn £50 or £60 a year. But the younger girls in less desirable situations still earned much the same as they would have thirty years earlier. It was not unheard of for a young kitchen maid or tweeny to earn five shillings a week or less in the twenties, and even an official enquiry into domestic service after the War, which proposed a number of improvements to the working conditions of servants, still recommended a wage for these young girls of only 7s 6d per week.

Of course, in judging these wage levels it has to be remembered that almost universally they were over and above the provision of board and lodging. Whether many servants would have chosen the board and lodging they received, though, is a different matter. The simple nature of many servants' rooms has already been mentioned. But even in terms of the provision of food, employers could be incredibly mean. Of course there were houses where the servants gorged themselves on the sumptuous leftovers of dinners upstairs. But all too often the servants had a totally different menu. Sometimes particularly mean

Those in service were expected to dress plainly, normally in a uniform prescribed by their employers. There were degrees of servants, too, often distinguished by differing uniforms.

employers even locked the store cupboards in which their own fare was kept to prevent the servants being tempted away from their own, less exciting and more meagre rations.

Indeed, in virtually all houses, no matter how enlightened the employer, servants were still largely regarded as objects, and seldom as human beings in their own right. In her book *Below Stairs*, Margaret Powell remembers her early morning chore of polishing the huge brass knob on the front door, only to find that by the time her employer came to inspect it, the cold of the dawn had tarnished the polished finish. Yet even such an obviously natural and unavoidable event was put down to the shortcomings of the servants.

Few employers were willing to allow any kind of laxity in the way their servants lived and behaved. Many regarded days off as an undesirable concession granted as rarely as possible. Unofficial trips out were very much frowned upon — in many establishments permission had to be sought even to make a short trip to a letter box, or to visit a doctor in cases of illness. Perks were few and far between, and often 'gifts' were of dubious benefit. It was not unheard of, for example, for a family's old clothes to be passed on to the servants, only for a sum of money to be docked from the next wage packet to cover the 'gift'.

It was not so much, though, that employers were consciously tyrannical. Most would have been horrified to think themselves so. Rather, even in the twenties, the years of rebellion against service, the monied classes took servants for granted. Indeed many regarded their employing of servants as almost a philanthropic act. Because there was so little real awareness of life in the lower echelons of society, many prosperous middle-class employers felt they provided girls and boys from humble backgrounds with the opportunity of exchanging a life of misery and degradation for a living in a respectable home in exchange for a good day's work.

It was perhaps in part this belief which led to the very strict routine of the servant's life, both at work itself and in the few leisure hours granted them each week. Except for days off, it was unusual for girls to be allowed out when work was over for a time, perhaps during the afternoon or late at night. Although here there was obviously the question of meeting boys (something dealt with at greater length later) many employers clearly felt that their servant establishment ought to be just that, and that any real degree of outside life was not to be encouraged.

Of course there were good, even exceptional, employers as well. Whilst many girls lived cramped in spartan attic rooms, some were given their own rooms, which were perhaps even decorated to their taste on arrival. Employers could be thoughtful as well as thought-less. Margaret Powell recalls one lady employer of hers, when she was working as a cook, who came down specially to the kitchen on the day of a large dinner party to say that the family would make do with a cold lunch as there would doubtless be a lot of work preparing for the evening. But such consideration seems generally to have been rare. And indeed if many women really did regard it as almost a privilege for their servants to be there, in their rich and respectable homes, such lack of thought is easily explicable.

The worst employers, without doubt, though, tended to be from the poorer end of respectable society, from those households which could only afford to maintain one or perhaps two young girls in general servant roles, and which nonetheless continued to try to maintain the airs and graces of the nobility, and demanded service to match. This left some poor young girl, badly paid and working long hours, to act as general maid doing all the cleaning, to be cook, and then turn out reasonably presentable to serve at table in the evenings. Once again, it is certain that even these employers were not consciously bad; their servants were simply a victim of the insatiable middle-class desire to emulate the ways of the aristocracy and of high society. Everything had to be just right, even if there was only one girl to do all the work to make it so.

Yet, even if a servant detested and loathed his or her employer, such feelings had to be suppressed if only for the sake of one's own future job prospects. This was because of the absolute role played by the written reference in the employment of new staff. Quite simply, no domestic servant would be employed if they had no character reference from a previous employer, unless of course they were starting at the bottom of the scale.

So, to leave a job in strained circumstances could be the total ruin of a servant. For many who displeased employers, perhaps by becoming pregnant which, whether at the hands of a member of the employing family, a guest, or an outsider, was always a cardinal sin. Often, girls who left in such circumstances were forced into prostitution to keep them and their baby. It could be particularly unfair, since it was often a son of the family who was responsible for seducing a young maid. But no matter. The fault was always hers, and dismissal a foregone conclusion.

Looking back, it is surprising to say the least that in reality servants not only seem to have accepted their lot but even did so with some degree of pleasure. There are, of course, those who look back to a time spent in service with displeasure and embarrassment. And, increasingly, after the War had ended, girls were refusing to surrender their independence to the way of life in the servant's hall. But even so, there seem to have been an equal number who genuinely enjoyed working in the homes of the wealthy who became trusted and loyal retainers, often remaining with a single family for the whole of their lives.

It still remained most young girls' objective to find a husband, though, and through him the way out of the servants hall. For many it remained an impossible dream. There were fewer men in service jobs, and in any case such a marriage probably meant a lifetime in service. And those errand boys who came to call could pick and choose from all the maids in the houses on their rounds. But there were days off, and not all were unlucky. Employers actively discouraged 'followers' because of the high staff turnover it might entail — but 'followers' there still were, and many became husbands. And that really was the only way back into the world they had come from.

This, then, was the world of the domestic servant in the twenties. But, like so much of British society in the postwar era, a process of evolution had begun which would change that world forever. The reason was simple: both the generation which had fought or which had driven trams, worked on the land and helped make munitions for the War effort, and the next, relatively liberated by changes of attitude within class and family, were less ready to countenance a life in service, waiting upon the needs of the prosperous. The 'servant problem' had arrived, and to stay.

After 1918, when both middle and upper-class families began to rebuild the establishments which had been dissipated by the needs of the War, and to re-create the lifestyle of the Indian summers before it, they found to their horror that for the first time ever their staff advertisements often went unanswered. It was perhaps their first real insight into the gulf that had opened up between them and their servants. Many women were genuinely surprised that fewer and fewer girls wanted that privilged opportunity of working away from their family background in a higher-class home. Suddenly, girls were unwilling to accept their alloted place in the social order. Amongst the upper classes the problem was viewed so seriously that the government promptly set up an official enquiry into it, an exercise that was repeated four years later in 1923. Although the Women's Advisory Committee, which carried out the first enquiry, was split by differing opinions and viewpoints, it did unanimously recognise that the reduction in the numbers of girls in service was due not just to the War but also to a growing distaste for the job. Eventually they recommended a shorter working day, better working conditions, fixed meal breaks and longer leisure time, including the revolutionary idea of annual leave. The Committee also suggested better training to help young girls adjust to the work, including, if possible, special domestic service schools.

In fact this last suggestion was acted upon, with the establishment of homecraft courses. But these were limited in scope, and did little to ease the servant problem. Equally, no one was willing to introduce Draconian legislation to impose philanthropy upon the servant-employing classes, and though many did make real efforts to make the lot of their servants better, in reality the general pattern changed little.

The employer class's mood of annoyance changed to one of fury after 1921 though, as unemployment began to rise. There was a torrent of letters to the press complaining about the shortage of domestic labour and demanding that, whilst this situation persisted, no women should receive the dole. The middle and upper classes saw it as being no more than the government's duty to take steps, however drastic, to force girls back into service.

Of course, no sensible government would have dared take such a step, particularly not at a time of relative political instability. But some individual local employment exchanges did do their best to deny the dole to girls who had been in service before the War in order to force them back to their old work. Even so, the fact remained that work in service was becoming a growing anathema to the working classes. Servants were 'stigmatised' as skiv-vies by the street communities from where they came. Girls told endless lies to cover up the fact that they were servants when they found the chance to meet a young man. There was a sizeable surplus of women, and hence they were at a great enough disadvantage without letting it be known that they belonged to a group increasingly regarded as inferior.

The background problem remained: the middle classes continued to aspire to greater things, and to try to live the life of high society, to do as it did, to talk as it talked, and to live as it lived. Many of them probably never even thought of a servant as another human being with similar feelings and desires to their own; they were no more than part of the chattels of being 'someone'.

But the War had inexorably, if to some invisibly, changed that. As the War to end all wars it had brought Britain together as a nation like it had never been brought together before. Until then, and throughout history, wars had been the playthings of an élite, fought between small armies, almost as duels of strength between two champions. The First World War was something completely new, and it broke the old order in two.

After 1918, there was a wave of nostalgia for the Edwardian era and for those who had lived it to the full. Society reformed itself, the Season began once more; people tried to act as if nothing had really changed. But there was no escaping the reality. The fabric of society itself had changed for good. Of course the servant girls were still born into the same working-class slum world, and this, together with the unemployment which was to bite so deeply during the next fifteen years, was the prime reason for much of the postwar dis-illusion. But at the end of the day people were no longer willing to accept that they had a set place in society. Some saw the way up as a matter of beating the middle classes at their own game — through self-improvement and by striving either to go themselves or to send their children to grammar schools and then perhaps even on to some form of higher education. Others were drawn to socialism, and often even to Bolshevism, to try to over-turn society completely. But whatever the bright young things of London society or the aspiring middle-class hostesses from the home counties may have wished, the world they hankered after was irretrievably lost.

The servant problem was eased by the enormous levels of unemployment in the late twenties and early thirties. Even the proudest preferred some income to the misery of life on the dole and in an unemployed society. But it was only temporary. Where cook had once baked the bread and the maids had done the washing, now the baker called regularly and the linen went to an outside laundry. Of course, there were still servants until well after 1945, and there remain a few today, though their status is much changed. But the world of the tweeny in the middle-class villa, of the landed gentry, and of the old ways, died with the flower of British youth in the carnage on Flanders field.

THE MIDDLE GROUND

It's almost impossible to find *the* archetypal member of the English middle class. Though regarded as a very definite social stratum in our society, it actually encompasses a wide range of people, many of whom have relatively little in common. A school teacher in an industrial city, or a prosperous artisan living away from the slum streets in a larger house with an inside lavatory would certainly have regarded themselves as middle class. But so would the owner of the local mill who lived in a huge town house and maintained a household with servants, and a governess for the children. The police inspector's family, who lived in a three-bedroomed house in the suburbs and employed a couple of maids, would also consider themselves middle class.

What they all had in common, though, was a desire to maintain that status which made them different from the working classes, to maintain a lifestyle and code of behaviour which made them better. The way to achieve this was to emulate their betters — to try to be like the rich and aristocractic. So having a servant, even if it was only one servant, was an important prerequisite. As well, one had to know how to behave, to understand etiquette, and to mix with all the right people. Those who found their way out of their working class background would often have very little, if anything, to do with relatives who still lived in the slum streets. A few even refused to acknowledge their ancestry.

Of course it would be wrong to assert that all middle class people were overt snobs. Many weren't. But that didn't stop them, for example, bringing up children so that they were well versed in social etiquette — how one ate one's soup, what to wear for particular occasions and so on. And many more were snobs and social climbers, trying desperately to get to know the right people, to be invited to the right parties, in general to win friends and influence people — to be someone who mattered. The teenage son of one middle-class family from the Midlands remembers his mother being advised by a friend: 'If you want to get on in your life, invite people to dinner who are above you. When you get to their level, drop them and, again, invite the people who're above you.'

One of the best identifications of class at that time was one's educational background. In life much store was still placed upon manners, and the way one behaved and spoke. To have been brought up and educated properly was a vital element in one's class progress. Furthermore, in the pre-television era, when conversation played a much more significant part in social life, what you could talk about was of great importance. Here again the quality of one's education was paramount, and the importance of the grammar school and the Sunday school as a 'way up' into middle-class respectability quite clear.

Additionally, the acquisition of a better education and of a more middle-class manner of living and behaving was vital for success in work. It was only natural that an employer would be better disposed towards a young man who spoke the same language in the same way and shared some of the same interests.

As a whole, the world in which the middle classes lived was a world apart from the life in the slums, although even this depended somewhat on the individual family. A third or fourth generation of a family that had made good would inevitably be better off than a family which had only just made the break. Even so, the comment of a doctor's daughter from Bolton probably sums up the difference best: 'in those days,' she said, 'everybody had a maid.' The middle classes tended to be more snobbish than the upper classes, particularly the remnants of the landed artisocracy. The middle classes tended to regard those lower down the social ladder as inferiors. Somehow the relations between the aristocracy and the people who worked on their estates managed to be less crude: they had a genuine respect for each other. But when the son of a Manchester coal miner called at the house of one of the middle-class members of his Sunday school, he was ordered to the tradesmen's entrance. Even though he vaguely knew the people who lived there, he was not, as a social inferior, entitled to use the front door.

Houses were much larger. A typical small middle-class home might be on two or three floors, with a kitchen and a drawing room, a couple of bedrooms, a bathroom, often a nursery and perhaps as well a small room in the attic for the maid or for a governess. The bathroom, unknown to the working classes, was a normal thing for the urban middle classes; the son of a Newcastle businessman said it never occurred to them as children that such luxuries were not universal. Facilities were much the same as one would find today, with tub, basin and lavatory. Kitchens were more universal, and the middle-class household cooked over a range as well. But as has been seen, in some lower-class homes mothers had to cook over an open coal fire.

The more prosperous lived in much larger homes, often in the large town houses still

Typical middle-class villas in a suburb of Leeds. Building boomed during the inter-war years, despite periods of recession. Houses such as this would have cost, in the 1930s, about £500 to £750.

The bathroom, unknown to the working classes, was a normal part of urban middle-class, as well as upper-class, life, made easier by the perfection of plumbing during the late-Victorian and Edwardian eras.

evident in most towns today, or out in the countryside within easy commuting distance of work. Here the number of servants would certainly be greater. A prosperous, professional middle-class family might employ a gardener, a cook, a chambermaid and a housemaid. In addition, where there were children in the family, most would also have a nanny and/or governess to take care of them.

Though the majority of women did not work, if they did not need to, few who could afford servants did much work in the home either. Sometimes the wife did do the cooking, and obviously if the family budget could not afford enough staff to do all that had to be done, then she would have to do more, but generally women avoided such tasks. One left such things to the servants, and it was almost a mark of social failure to those who did care about such things, if they had to. Interestingly it was out in the countryside where this norm was most often broken, and particularly on the farms. Perhaps because the whole family was used to mucking in on the farm, however prosperous, the women tended to work far more than their urban counterparts.

Instead, middle-class women from the suburbs or the towns and cities tended to spend a lot of their time socialising and very often engaged in charitable work. This might consist of organising charitable functions to raise money for needy causes, or helping out on a more practical basis, whether throwing a tea party for the local Sunday school children or going off into the East End of London to help the needy. Other parts of their spare time might be spent reading or doing crochet, perhaps playing tennis with friends or taking music lessons.

But as the decade progressed, more and more women had to take an active role in running their homes. As we have seen in the earlier chapter on servants, it was becoming more and more difficult to get the right staff, and to afford to keep as many as were really needed to run the home. Moreover, household work was becoming a little easier. There were now a few mechanical household gadgets on the market — most notably the earliest electric vacuum cleaners — which were to reduce the domestic workload, and to make it less painful for women to make the break from having servants to do all the work. Even so, most middle-class families still had servants to do their work right through the 1920s, even if perhaps they could now only afford to pay the wages of one or two maids rather than three and a cook.

Within the middle-class family can be found a very clear example of the relative confusion that arises when one tries too hard to define class in an absolute manner. Virtually universally among the working classes, or at least among the lower echelons of society, the household was dominated by the father of the family. Equally, within the upper-class household, it was usually the women who ran the family. But for the middle classes there was no hard-and-fast rule. The household of a Newcastle businessman, for example, might be very much run by his wife — he was preoccupied with work for much of the time. But a Bolton doctor could be absolute head of the household, and his family fitted in with his wishes and rules.

But if one does seek a trend, then it seems that where a family could clearly be seen to be social climbers, it was usually the woman who organised everything. It was she who employed the servants, who held the dinner parties and the 'At Homes', and who strove to see that everything was done just right. Her husband almost certainly had little time to spare from his work to do anything other than attend the events organised by his wife, or the functions to which they were in turn invited.

Often the middle-class snobbery and desire to impress could be taken to ridiculous extremes. There were women who severely reprimanded servants for forgetting to put the morning paper or the toast onto a silver salver before bringing it upstairs or into breakfast. Many led strictly regimented lives — far more so, in fact, than the class they were trying to emulate. Dinner was always at a set hour, and woe betide children who were late, if indeed they were allowed to dine with their parents. Many weren't, and ate in the nursery or in the kitchen instead. One had to dress for dinner — not to do so was considered very bad form, and certainly not what was expected of one.

Others arranged visits to events such as Ascot, perhaps only just to say that they had been somewhere that society had also gone, or to catch a glimpse of the people they were trying to emulate.

But not everybody was that bad. Most middle-class families tended to be not dissimilar to those of today, though young people were a little more restricted than is now the case. The family unit was fairly strong, and tended to socialise as a unit as well.

It was, for example, not particularly common for the children of a middle-class family to be left alone to hold parties or to get together with friends, except if they went out for an evening at the theatre or a concert. And even then, as in working-class homes, rules were strict. A firm father might be furious — if not actually violent as in the slums — if a daughter returned late from an evening out with friends or, particularly, with a young man. Of course there were parties for the young, but these tended to be held by parents on behalf of their children rather than by the children alone. Family parties were also a common form of entertainment among the middle classes, where people of all ages mixed together.

Music and the theatre were generally more popular than the cinema among the middle classes, though younger people tended to be just as eager as anyone for the developing delights of the cinema. But none of these was a very common pastime for most people, particularly if they lived in a commuter area. Instead they entertained a great deal, holding regular dinner parties, and women tended to hold lunch or coffee parties during the day while their husbands were at work.

Indeed, one of the main restraints on the social life of a family, with the exception of the young during the school holidays, was the amount of time that most men spent working, particularly if they were in business on their own account. This was particularly true for the large number of mill owners and merchants who were constantly occupied seeking business in an era of economic difficulty. Very often the father of the family simply wasn't there, and many children saw little of their fathers while growing up.

Of course, the majority of children from more prosperous middle-class backgrounds were sent away to school, and even where they went to the local grammar school there was still homework to be done. So that during the year, it was only when holidays came rund that they were free to enjoy themselves a little.

But, as in upper-class families, most middle-class children from well-off families were brought up by nursemaids or nannies. Parents tended to be too busy, the father working, the mother socialising, to pay too much attention to their offspring. Indeed, it was fairly common for younger children to be presented to their parents for only a few minutes at a certain time of day. Since many of the nannies were strict and uncaring, young life could often be a lonely and unhappy affair.

It was not always that bad, of course. It did depend very much upon the social perceptions of a particular family. Less well-off though comfortable parents who did not have the burning ambition of many to better themselves, paid much closer attention to the development of their children, and were little different from the parents of today.

It is probably fair to say that the English middle classes have always been the most consistent churchgoers and the most religious members of society as a whole in recent times. This was particularly true in the late eighteenth and early nineteenth centuries when, at a time when church attendance was falling, the nonconformist elements of northern England in particular formed the backbone of the commercial middle classes. And it was certainly at least in part due to this that Britain was so successful economically. The Quaker and Methodist families were very often the mill and factory owners who worked long hours and hard, as they believed God expected them to, to turn their businesses into world beaters.

By the First World War there is no doubt that the great era of the nonconformist middle classes was over, and that the influence of religion had waned very dramatically. Though there were still traces of it left, particularly in the north-west. When conscription was advocated during the First World War, those who came out against it and fought bitterly to prevent it did so on the grounds that it was immoral to make men whose religious views banned them from fighting defy those beliefs and join the army, and that conscription would damage business by removing much of its labour force. It was noticeable that that advocates of these arguments tended to be the same men.

So it would be wrong to say that the decline in religious belief and attendance was universal across the classes, or at least to the same extent. There were still large numbers of nonconformist middle-class families — and for that matter Church of England families — who were strict attenders of church, chapel or Sunday school on a Sunday morning. Even so, though, the working classes were not alone in having far greater leisure opportunities on a Sunday, and many who had always gone to church began to drift away from further attendance if only because their faith was not strong enough to overcome the attraction of the other things that there were to do.

Here the arrival of the motor car was important. In the years after the war most middle-class families who were reasonably prosperous bought their first car, and took advantage of it to take long excursions at weekends. In the same way that the advent of the tram had opened up new vistas for the working classes at the turn of the century, so the motor car did the same for the more prosperous classes in the years after the First World War.

In the field of leisure another factor also differentiated the middle and upper classes, namely their holidays. Though there was some coincidence in that people from all walks of life who could afford it went to Scotland fishing, otherwise there tended to be greater differences. Society people went off to Paris or Vienna, to Cannes or Biarritz; the doctor or town solicitor and his family went to resorts like Llandudno.

But as the decade passed, there came clearer evidence of the fine dividing line between middle and upper class, and indeed between lower and middle class. Before the War the family depending upon a weekly wage from the mill or factory had never been away for holidays. Now as its living standard improved, so such previously unheard of luxuries became possible. As one resort began to attract more working-class people so the middle classes who had always tended to go there began looking elsewhere — this being one reason for the popularity among the middle classes of towns like Llandudno which were a little further away from the main population centres. And as the twenties passed, it became more usual for middle-class families to make the trip over to the continent themselves, following the time-honoured example of the upper class.

Statistically, after the First World War, England was becoming much more middle class. There was a trend in population away from the old industrial areas, and a corresponding growth in the suburban areas of the Home Counties. Middle-class occupations expanded on several fronts. Firstly the War had hastened the increase in size of the bureaucracy

Although, by the 1920s, it was becoming more normal for working-class people to go away on holiday each year, most of those who gathered on the beaches came from the middle classes.

148

which served government, and this continued in the twenties with the introduction of complex social legislation such as the extension of the dole to a far wider range of working people. Such changes needed more administrators to control them. Also as many of the old family businesses declined or moved into the hands of the second or third generation of the families that had founded them in the prosperous mid-Victorian era, or perhaps even before, so the need for managers to run the business on a day-to-day level increased. The new generation of manager was different. The men who worked all the hours that God gave were no longer the norm. Instead it was becoming more common for industry to take on professional managers to run areas such as production, sales and marketing.

But whilst the country was becoming more middle class, it remained hard to distinguish the middle ground, socially, from the near edges of the two extremes. There was little difference between the small town shopkeeper and his working-class customer. Equally the most prosperous middle classes were now enjoying a lifestyle little different from that of many aristocratic families. The introduction into London society of the hard-faced men who looked to have done well out of the War served only to blur this distinction further.

One thing can be said with confidence, though: the middle class was without doubt the most status-conscious group in society as a whole. It was from their number that the worst social climbers came, who paid most attention to what they saw as the way to behave. They were trying to conform to the rather intangible concept of the done thing. They wanted to be ladies and gentlemen, and recognised as such.

The nineteenth century, with its rapid industrial expansion, saw a corresponding growth in the numbers of the middle classes — those who found status not through birth but through their own enterprise. The twentieth has seen a similar growth, but not of the commercial middle classes. This has been the age of the middle manager and the bureaucrat, and as an age it was born with the demolition of the old order by the First World War.

By 1918 the era of the British aristocracy was over, and their place at the head of the nation passed to the wealthiest members of the commercial classes. At the same time more and more people began to break away from the undermass, to find greater wealth and security in the ranks of the swelling suburban middle classes. In 1918 that break away was still only a trickle, but as the years and decades passed that trickle turned into a flood. The First World War didn't change Britain overnight, nor did it end with the creation of a land fit for heroes to live in. But by the time the final shots were fired, the seeds of a new era were well and truly sown.

POSTSCRIPT

Almost all of this book is based on the reminiscences of some fifty people, chosen to be as good as possible a cross-section, both socially and geographically, of England after the First World War. I have deliberately chosen not to name them in the text, both because some, for whatever reason, didn't really want me to, and also because I am far from convinced that using names actually adds anything to a book like this, which is intended to be more a portrait of an era than an oral history text.

However, that said, I owe the reader some more detailed explanation of the kind of people whose memories make up this book. I set off with the intention of finding people from as many walks of life as possible, and have tried to make sure that the interview material covered most of the country. Inevitably, everyone I talked to was fairly young in the years after the War — the oldest were in their twenties. Happily, all were very lucid and their memories mostly very exact and definite.

Those interviewed for the first section of the book, on life in the large towns and cities, included a distinguished local historian from Salford who was brought up in a two-up-two-down during the First World War and was at grammar school in the early 1920s. I also talked, amongst others, to a woman who was at elementary school, also in Salford, after the War, to a newly-wed housewife from Birmingham, to a girl who left school in a village just outside Bradford at the end of the War, and went to work in the mill, before becoming a clerk in a shipping company. I went to see former colliery workers, one of them a junior manager, from the Lancashire, Cheshire and Nottinghamshire coalfields. I spoke to a railway offical from Exeter, a postal worker from Reading and spent an afternoon with an old people's club in the East End of London, talking both to people brought up locally, and others from other parts of the country, particularly Bristol and the North-East.

My country reminiscences came from various sources. I spoke to an old farm worker from Sussex, a farmer's son from Coleshill in the Midlands, and also used an archive tape of an old farm worker from Rossendale in Lancashire. I also used the reminiscences of a smallholder's daughter from Sussex, a priest who was at the time working in the Potteries and the countryside around, a gamekeeper on the Grosvenor estates near Chester, and of the colliery manager mentioned earlier, who lived in a country village on the edge of Derbyside. Town memories came, among others, from the son of a businessman from Long Eaton near Nottingham, and from a gardener's daughter from Cambridge.

To find out more about society life I went to see the son of a baronet who was both a successful businessman and MP. The son began work in the City in the early twenties before rejoining the family business. I spoke to a former deb, whose father was chairman of one of London's most famous department stores. I also spoke to the son of a Newcastle shipyard owner who was able to offer memories both of his own middle-class upbringing and of the life of his uncle who mixed in high society circles. I spoke to a former Conservative minister who was at Eton during the 1920s, and to the young wife of an Oxford don elected soon after 1918. Further public school memories were provided by the daughter of a GP from Bolton who went to Cheltenham Ladies College after the War.

There was, of course, considerable interplay between topics, since many of those I talked to were able to offer a wide range of memories. These have been supplemented with a few written memoirs, some archive material, including a series of reminiscences broadcast on BBC radio in the 1950s. I also made some use of contemporary magazines, particularly the *Sketch* and the *Tatler*.

PICTURE ACKNOWLEDGMENTS

BBC Hulton Picture Library: pages 26, 92, 98, 114 (top and bottom), 115, 119, 120, 124, 129 (top and bottom)

Greater London Record Office and Library, GLC: page 44 (top and bottom)

Museum of London: page 46

The Illustrated London News Picture Library (the *Sketch*): pages 50, 108, 116, 145

National Portrait Gallery, London: pages 59, 66

Institute of Agricultural History and Museum of English Rural Life, University of Reading: page 89